Kirtley Library
Columbia College
8th and Rogers
Columbia, MO. 65201

YORKSHIRE LEGENDS
AND TRADITIONS

This is a volume in the Arno Press collection

INTERNATIONAL FOLKLORE

Advisory Editor
Richard M. Dorson

Editorial Board
Issachar Ben Ami
Vilmos Voigt

*See last pages of this volume
for a complete list of titles*

YORKSHIRE
Legends and Traditions

THOMAS PARKINSON

ARNO PRESS
A New York Times Company
New York / 1977

Editorial Supervision: LUCILLE MAIORCA

Reprint Edition 1977 by Arno Press Inc.

Reprinted from a copy in
 The University of Illinois Library

INTERNATIONAL FOLKLORE
ISBN for complete set: 0-405-10077-9
See last pages of this volume for titles.

Manufactured in the United States of America

Library of Congress Cataloging in Publication Data

Parkinson, Thomas.
   Yorkshire legends and traditions.

   (International folklore)
   Reprint of the 1888 ed. published by E. Stock, London.
   Includes index.
   1. Folk-lore--England--Yorkshire. 2. Legends--
England--Yorkshire. I. Title. II. Series.
GR142.Y5P3 1977   390'.09428'1   77-70615
ISBN 0-405-10117-1

YORKSHIRE LEGENDS AND TRADITIONS.

YORKSHIRE
Legends and Traditions

AS TOLD BY HER ANCIENT CHRONICLERS,
HER POETS, AND JOURNALISTS.

BY THE

REV. THOMAS PARKINSON, F.R.Hist.S.,

MEMBER OF THE SURTEES SOCIETY,
THE YORKSHIRE ARCHÆOLOGICAL AND TOPOGRAPHICAL ASSOCIATION,
VICAR OF NORTH OTTERINGTON.

> 'History hath no page
> More brightly lettered of heroic dust,
> Or manly worth, or woman's nobleness,
> Than thou may'st show; thou hast nor hill nor dale,
> But lives in legend.'

LONDON:
ELLIOT STOCK, 62, PATERNOSTER ROW, E.C.
1888.

'*We marked each memorable scene,
And held poetic talk between;
Nor hill nor brook we paced along,
But had its legend or its song.*'
SCOTT.

INTRODUCTION.

LEGEND, from the Latin *legendum*, a thing to be read, is a word which covers a wide field (even when limited by the bounds of a single county) for a writer to undertake to reap, and present the harvest to his readers. The ordinary acceptance, however, of the term somewhat further limits it to those stories and narratives which hang between history and fable,—to tales of superstition, of marvel, and of credulity.

Very closely connected with legend is another field of much interest—viz., that of tradition (*traditum*, a thing handed down); and to avoid having to draw a line where the one continually runs into the other, and so to distinguish between legend and tradition—where the distinction is often very slight indeed—the author has joined the two in the title given to this collection, 'Yorkshire Legends and Traditions.' Under this title the reader will, therefore, find stories and narratives ranging from those which border upon authentic history, and have undoubtedly fact for their foundation, to others whose origin can only have been superstition or fable, and many of them handed down from the mythical gods and heroes of heathen days.

While there will be also found a middle class, consisting of relations in which it is possible to perceive a centre of fact or historical truth, but rendered indefinite and indistinct by the halo of mystery or perversion with which time, or ingenuity, has surrounded it.

Many of the mythical legends, and legends and traditions of the marvellous, found in Yorkshire, are, of course, by no means peculiar to the county. On the contrary, they are—some or other of them—found related of places and of persons far apart in situation and time.

Such stories, wherever found, have always had a fascination for the young; and, told from father to son, in the long evenings of winter, in the farmhouses of remote valleys and moorsides, they have formed an *unwritten* literature, long before they found embodiments in more permanent forms. They have seized upon the fancy, and given scope to the imagination, of men in all ages. Poets and painters especially have revelled amid the fields of legend and tradition. In every art-gallery—whether of ancient or modern works—legends and traditions of every kind are found embodied on canvas of every size; while many of the finest poems of our language—such as 'The Idylls of the King,' or 'The White Doe of Rylstone'—owe their inspiration to Arthurian or local legends or traditions. The extent to which art and poetry are thus indebted to legend and tradition will appear to the reader as he turns over the pages of this collection. In a great majority of instances, either references are made to poems, to which the subjects have given rise, or, as is often the case, the author has allowed the story to be told in the words of the poets themselves.

The writer is not aware of any similar collection of legends and traditions of his native county having been made before. He has laid under contribution almost every variety of source of information. Especially is he indebted to Dixon's 'Stories of Craven Dales,' and to several local weekly journals—the *Yorkshire Post, Leeds Mercury,* and others. The collection has been growing under his hand for several years, and by no means exhausts the field. Should a reading public appreciate and encourage this effort of bringing together these sheaves from the romance and the marvellous of this county of 'broad acres,' another wain-load of the same kind, already collected, will probably be sent forth in due time.

CONTENTS.

I.

LEGENDS AND TRADITIONS CONNECTED WITH THE EARLY HISTORY OF YORKSHIRE.

	PAGE
THE ORIGIN OF THE NAME 'YORK'	1
GREGORY OF ROME AND THE YOUTHS FROM DEIRA	3
PAULINUS IN NORTHUMBRIA	4
THE JORDAN OF ENGLAND	7
FOUNDATION OF YORK MINSTER	7
RAGNAR LODBROG AND CRAKE CASTLE	8
WHY BUERN THE BUSECARLE BROUGHT THE DANES INTO YORKSHIRE, 867 A.D.	10
DEATH OF ELLA, KING OF BERNICIA, NEAR YORK	14
ELLSWORTH AND ELLE-CEOSS	17
THE DANES IN YORKSHIRE AND ST. ALKELDA OF MIDDLEHAM	19
A NORMAN ARMY STOPPED NEAR NORTHALLERTON BY FEAR OF ST. CUTHBERT	20

II.

LEGENDS AND TRADITIONS OF ABBEYS AND OF MONASTIC LIFE.

WHITBY ABBEY	22
ST. HILDA'S WORMS	23
THE OBEISANCE OF BIRDS	24
CÆDMON THE POET	24
THE HERMIT OF ESKDALE—A BROTHER OF WHITBY	27
WHITBY ABBEY BELLS	29
FOUNTAINS ABBEY	29

Contents.

	PAGE
RIEVAULX ABBEY AND KIRKHAM PRIORY:	
WALTER DE ESPEC	31
WALTER DE ESPEC AT THE BATTLE OF THE STANDARD	33
A PRIOR OF KIRKHAM'S HORSE	36
THE ABBEY OF MEAUX OR MELSA	37
BOLTON PRIORY	40
FOUNDATION OF THE PRIORY, AND THE BOY OF EGREMOND	40
'THE BOY OF EGREMOND'	44
THE WHITE DOE OF RYLSTONE	45
BARNOLDSWICK AND KIRKSTALL ABBEYS	59
MARY, THE MAID OF THE INN	62
ORIGIN OF SELBY ABBEY	65
THE GRAY PALMER AND HYLDA, THE NUN OF NUN-APPLETON	66
ROCHE ABBEY	70
LEGENDS CONNECTED WITH ST. JOHN OF BEVERLEY	72
A LEGEND OF WATTON NUNNERY	73
PUCH, THE EARL, OF SOUTH BURTON	75
THE TWO SISTERS OF BEVERLEY	76
EARL ADDI'S SERVANT, OF NORTH BURTON	79
THE SHRINE OF ST. JOHN OF BEVERLEY AND THE PLEDGED SWORD	80
LEGENDS CONNECTED WITH ST. WILLIAM OF YORK	86
THE BROKEN BRIDGE	91
EYES GIVEN TO THE BLIND	92
THE ORDEAL OF FIRE	93
SIGHT GIVEN TO A BLIND GIRL	94
THE YOUNG STUDENT	95
THE HORN OF ULPHUS	96
A LEGEND OF ST. CUTHBERT AND RIPON MONASTERY	101
LEGENDS OF ST. ROBERT, THE HERMIT OF KNARESBOROUGH	104

III.

LEGENDS OF SATANIC AGENCY.

THE DEVIL'S ARROWS OR BOLTS	115
SITES OF CHURCHES	119
THUMB-MARKS ON THE HADDOCK	121
THE DEVIL'S BRIDGE	121
THE DEVIL'S APRONFUL	124

IV.

BARGEST AND GHOST LEGENDS.

	PAGE
THE BARGEST OF THE TROLLER'S GILL	126
THE BARGEST, NEAR GRASSINGTON	129
THE BOSKY DIKE BOGGART	131
THE APPEARANCE OF BARGEST A PRESAGE OF DEATH:	
THE WISE WOMAN OF LITTONDALE	134
THE GHOST AT TRINITY CHURCH, YORK	140

V.

LEGENDS AND TRADITIONS OF MOTHER SHIPTON.

MOTHER SHIPTON—HER BIRTH, LIFE, AND DEATH	151
MOTHER SHIPTON'S PROPHECIES	156
THE PROPHECY OF MOTHER SHIPTON IN THE REIGN	
OF KING HENRY VIII.	158
APOCRYPHAL SAYINGS	164

VI.

LEGENDS OF DRAGONS AND OTHER SERPENTINE MONSTERS.

TENURE OF THE MANOR OF SOCKBURN	167
THE SERPENT OF HANDALE	168
THE WORM OF SEXHOW	169
THE DRAGON OF LOSCHY WOOD	170
THE SERPENT OF SLINGSBY	172
THE DRAGON OF WANTLEY	173

VII.

LEGENDS AND TRADITIONS OF BATTLES AND BATTLE-FIELDS.

THE WHITE BATTLE OF MYTON	178
THE BATTLE OF BOROUGHBRIDGE	181
THE BATTLE OF WAKEFIELD	184
THE BATTLE OF TOWTON	187
THE ROSES OF TOWTON MOOR	191
MARSTON MOOR FIGHT	194
CROMWELL AND SIR R. GRAHAM	195
CROMWELL AT RIPLEY	196
ANOTHER STORY	197
CAPTAIN LISTER: BATTLE OF TADCASTER, 1642	198

	PAGE
'PITY POOR BRADFORD.' A LEGEND OF THE CIVIL WAR TIMES -	198

VIII.

LEGENDS OF WELLS, LAKES, ETC.

THE EBBING AND FLOWING WELL AT GIGGLESWICK	204
LADY WELLS	205
ST. HELEN'S WELL	206
ST. JOHN'S WELL AT HARPHAM	207
THE DRUMMING WELL AT HARPHAM	207
WORDSWORTH'S HART-LEAP WELL	209
THE LEGEND OF SEMERWATER	214
GORMIRE	218

IX.

MISCELLANEOUS LEGENDS, ETC.

THE SWINE HARRIE; OR, 'HOIST ON HIS OWN PETARD'	219
UPSALL AND ITS CROCKS OF GOLD	221
HAVERAH PARK.—A LAME LEGEND	223
A WILD BOAR LEGEND	224
DE LACY AND LORD DACRE'S DAUGHTER	225
THE BEGGAR'S OR LOVER'S BRIDGE AT EGTON	227
THE BEGGAR'S BRIDGE	228
THE WHITE HORSE OF THE STRID, OR THE THREE SISTERS OF BEAMSLEY	229
OSMOTHERLEY	233
THE GIANT OF SESSAY	235
WADDA OF MULGRAVE, AND BELL, HIS WIFE	239

LEGENDS OF YORKSHIRE.

I.

LEGENDS AND TRADITIONS CONNECTED WITH THE EARLY HISTORY OF YORKSHIRE.

THE ORIGIN OF THE NAME 'YORK.'

THE origin of the name *York*, or Roman *Eboracum*, from which the *shire* derives its cognomen, is buried in obscurity, and, like most things obscure, it has gathered around it many legendary and traditional stories.

The chronicler Geoffrey of Monmouth is responsible for more than one of these stories. He relates how a colony of Trojans, under a leader named Brute, conquered Albion, and, settling on the Thames, built there the city of Troja Nova, now London, and gave the new name Brutaine, or Britain, to the country, about 1100 B.C. The third king, according to the same authority, of Troja Nova was Mempricus. A son of Mempricus was named Ebraucus, and he, journeying northwards, founded the city on the banks of the Ouse, called from him Kaer-Ebrauc, or the City of Ebraucus. This took place, says the old writer, 'about the time that David reigned in Judea, Sylvius Latinus in Italy, and that Gad, Nathan and Asaph prophesied in Israel, which epoch falls A.M. 2983 or B.C. 983.'

Ebraucus also, we are told, built two other cities in the north, one said to have been Aldborough, and the other named 'Mount Agned,' or the Mount of Sorrow; also 'The Maiden's Castle,' but now Edinburgh. He reigned sixty years, and by twenty wives had twenty sons and thirty daughters, all of whose names are duly chronicled, and then died, at an extreme old age, and was buried in the city which he had founded, and where he had reigned and flourished so long, Caer-Ebrauc.

Another story, as to the origin of York, is to the effect that a colony of Gauls settled in Spain, but, being compelled to move on from there, by the Carthaginians or Romans, took possession first of Ireland, then of Central England, and built York, naming the city Eboracum, from Ebora, a town in Portugal, or from Ebura in Andalusia, whence they had come.

Another tradition is that the Britons were themselves the founders of the city, giving it the name of Caer-Efroc, or the City of the Wild Boars. Efroc, shortened to Efer, or Evor, and Wic, a retreat or dwelling, being added, we get Evor-wic or Ebor-wic, hence both Eboracum and York ('Vor-wic). As confirmation of this it is added that the Forest of Galtres (Gautes, wild boars), came up very nearly to the city gates.

There is yet another traditional derivation of the name. The name of Aldborough, the capital of the Brigantines, near Boroughbridge, was formerly Iseur, Latinized Isurium. Near this place two rivers—or rather a river and a rivulet—the Ure and the Ouse—unite, and, taking the name of the smaller, form the well-known Ouse. In primitive times one of these bore the name of the Isis, and the other that of the Eure; and the city founded at the junction was designated from their united names 'Is-eur,' or Isurium. In course of time Iseur fell into decay and dropped out of history, while the rising city on the banks of the Ouse, but a few miles lower down, usurped its name and place in story. Iseur, in colloquial language, soon for brevity became 'Yeur,' and this, with the addition of 'Wic,' gave us Yeur-wic and then York.

In this latter story is probably to be found the germ of the true origin of the name; only that it came from the river Ure directly, and not through Isurium, being simply *'Ure,'* or *'Yore,'* and *'Wic.'* The other stories of the derivation of the name and origin of the city, and so of the county's designation, must be left to the reader to give to them the position he pleases in the region of history, legend, or tradition.

GREGORY OF ROME AND THE YOUTHS FROM DEIRA.

In the middle of the sixth century, Ella, or Ida, a leader of the tribe of the Angles, took possession of what is now Yorkshire and South Durham, and founded the kingdom of Deira, whose capital stood probably where Market Weighton or Beverley now stands. The name *Deira*, the land of the deer, indicates the condition of the country at that time.

However well known already, it is almost impossible to omit, in a collection of legends and traditions of Yorkshire, the story of the Monk Gregory and the youths from Deira in the slave-market at Rome. Without it, such a collection would be defective.

It was some years after the foundation of the kingdom of Deira that Gregory, walking through the slave-market of the Imperial city, had his attention arrested by the fair complexions, flaxen hair, and well-formed limbs of certain youths exposed for sale. They were, what we should now term Yorkshire lads, from the kingdom of Deira. Gregory paused, and asked of what race they were? He was told that they were Angles. Fond of making a play upon words of a similar sound, he replied: 'Ah! they are fit to be made angels. From what province do they come?' he continued. 'From the kingdom of Deira,' was the response. 'Ah, then,' said he, 'they must be freed *de ira*,' that is, from the anger of God. 'Who is their king?' he next inquired. 'Ella,' was the answer. 'Then, indeed, they must be taught to sing Alleluia.' And from this time, we are told, Gregory determined to come as a missionary to this country. He was frustrated in his intention by being raised to be Bishop of Rome; but ultimately he sent, under a monk named Augustine, who was joined by Paulinus, Justus, and others, a mission, which arrived, not in our own northern Deira, but in Kent, in 596 A.D.

PAULINUS IN NORTHUMBRIA.

Kent and its king soon became Christian, but it was some thirty years or more before the missionaries could find the opportunity to enter Yorkshire. The occasion at last presented itself.

Edwin, the young King of Deira, after many vicissitudes, had united to his kingdom the more northern one of Bernicia, and was now (*i.e.* 625) first King of Northumbria. He sought in marriage Ethelburg, a daughter of the King of Kent. She was, of course, as were her parents, a Christian. Edwin was yet a heathen; and consent to the marriage was only given on the condition that the princess should be accompanied to her husband's court by a bishop or clergyman to act as her chaplain, and provide her, and those who accompanied her, with the rites of the Christian religion. It was determined that Paulinus, one of the missionaries, should thus accompany Ethelburga. This was in the year 625. Paulinus of course made use of his opportunities to propagate the Gospel; and some two years afterwards the king, moved by a series of providential deliverances vouchsafed to him, and by the exhortations of the queen's chaplain, called together the Witenagemot, or great council of the kingdom, of Northumbria, to consider this new faith taught among them.

This council was held at, or in the neighbourhood of, Market Weighton. Paulinus first preached to the assembled nobles the doctrines of the Christian faith. The king then asked each noble in turn what he thought of these doctrines. The first to reply was Coifi, the high priest of the god Woden, whose temple was at Godmundingham, a village close by where they were assembled. The substance of Coifi's reply was that he was anxious to know more clearly what the new doctrines were, for he had long come to the conclusion that there was no reality or good in the service of the gods whom they worshipped, and, if the king liked the new religion better, by all means let it be adopted.

The next speaker was a nobleman, who said: 'It seems to me, O king, that this life of ours may be likened to a bird, which, when you and your nobles are sitting at supper in your great hall, enters the room by a lattice at one end, and flying through, passes out at the opposite end. It comes out of darkness, it passes through the light and warm room, and out again into darkness. Whence it came none can say, nor whither it has gone. So what comes before this life, and what after it, is enveloped in darkness. If the new doctrine will tell us anything of it, it is what we want.'

Others expressed like views, and Coifi again arose and asked that Paulinus should further explain what he taught. This Paulinus did; and then the heathen priest once more got up, and said, 'I have long known, O king, that there was nothing in our religion; for the more I sought for good in it, the less I found it. And here I freely confess that in this new preaching I find the good which there I could not find. Let us make haste to abjure and burn the altars which we have consecrated to such poor purpose.' There and then the king and nobles accepted the new faith.

'Who,' asked Edwin, 'will set about to destroy the idols?' 'None so fit as I,' replied Coifi. 'I taught the people to worship them. I will be the first to destroy them.' He called for a spear and a war-horse, both forbidden things to a priest. He mounted, and galloped up Godmundingham Lane, and rode full tilt at the temple door. The common people thought him mad. He pierced the door again and again with his spear, and then called on the persons who had congregated to finish the work of destruction which he had thus begun. Then they hewed down the doors, and burned the temple and all that it contained. Now, and for long, the Parish Church of Godmanham has stood, and yet stands, on the site of the Temple of Woden.

THE JORDAN OF ENGLAND.

After Edwin's baptism the work of conversion went quickly on in all parts of the country. The king had what we might call a summer residence at Catterick, in Swaledale. Thither Paulinus, now bishop, frequently accompanied him, and on one occasion, during a visit of thirty-six days, so says Bede, the bishop spent the whole of the time catechising the people and baptizing them in the Swale. Ten thousand were baptized on one day! On this account the Swale has since been called in legend and tradition 'The Jordan of England.'

FOUNDATION OF YORK MINSTER.

On Easter Day, April 12th, A.D. 627, Edwin, the King of Northumbria, was baptized. The place selected for the ceremony was what is now the City of York. There the king built, for the occasion, a small wooden church, which he caused to be dedicated to St. Peter. After the ceremony he commanded a larger one of stone to be commenced on the spot. This was done, but Edwin, unfortunately, did not live to finish it, but on that spot has stood a Christian Church ever since, represented now by the Minster, still dedicated to St. Peter, and of which all Yorkshiremen are so justly proud.

RAGNAR LODBROG AND CRAKE CASTLE.

So far back as the days of the Saxon and the Dane, there stood, on the well-known prominent hill beyond Easingwold, the Castle of Crake—or Crec, as it was then called. Though situated in the Saxon kingdom of Deira, it belonged, at the time of our story, to Ella, King of Bernicia, the more northern division of Northumbria. It had previously been given to St. Cuthbert, the well-known northern saint, as a resting-place on his long journey from Lindisfarne to the south; but Ella, who had little respect either for religion or for right, had seized upon it, and converted it into a fortress in his neighbour's domains, and its underground dungeons into a prison for those whom he wished to hide from the world.

About the same period there was reigning in the Danish islands a noted king named Ragnar Lodbrog. None of their ancient kings is more celebrated in Scandinavian poetry than Ragnar. His queen was a shepherdess, celebrated for beauty and song, whom he found on the Norwegian mountains. Troubles, however, arose, and Ragnar was driven from his kingdom. As was usual in those times, he fitted up a war-ship, and, with a number of followers such as himself, started off to find another home, and establish another kingdom, wherever the fates should lead him. He landed on the coasts of Bernicia, near Bamborough; and before Ella the king could collect his forces to oppose him, he desolated, with the usual ferocity and cruelty of the Danes, the farmsteads and villages in the vicinity. Still, according to the notions of the times, a grand and noble old Dane was he. But at length Ella came upon his small band with a larger force, and nearly annihilated it. Ragnar, however, had not the fortune to fall in the fight. He was taken prisoner. Ella spared none who had offended him; and his royal prisoner he sent off to his remote inland stronghold at Crake, that he might there wreak his revenge on the invader of Bernicia, and set an example of the vengeance which other northern Vikings might expect if they set foot in Ella's domains. The dungeon beneath the old castle at Crake was furnished with snakes, and vipers, and venomous and loathsome reptiles of every kind, for the purpose of torture and death. The entrance was a round hole in its roof. To this the unfortunate Ragnar was brought. He was divested of his clothing, and then, by means of a rope, lowered into the horrible pit: then drawn up again for the gratification of his tormentor, and taunted, and bid to beg for mercy. Instead of which, he cursed the Saxon king, and rejoiced in the assurance that those would come from Denmark who would avenge their kinsman's cruel death, and slay his oppressor, and that his own greatest gratification, in the great hereafter, would be to drink out of the skull of Ella at the banqueting-tables of Odin in the halls of Valhalla. With these words on his lips, he was lowered again into the place of death. And so died the old Scandinavian heathen warrior and king in the Castle of Crake.

Lodbrog's death-song, ascribed usually to Austaga, his widowed queen, is among the best and most popular of the Scandinavian *sagas*, or ancient poetry. Hinga, and Hubba, and Bruen, his three sons, as the old warrior had foreseen, avenged his death. They came with their hordes up the Humber, laid siege to York, and first defeated Ella's ally, Osbert, and then Ella himself. One account says they took Ella captive, and ordered him to be flayed alive. The complete conquest of the country followed; the sceptre of the whole of Northumbria passed from Saxon to Danish hands. In this story we have, no doubt, legend, tradition, and historic truth mingled together, and it requires the knowledge and acumen of a Freeman or a Stubbs to disentangle them.

Why Buern the Busecarle brought the Danes into Yorkshire, 867 A.D.

The legend as to the descent of the Danes upon Northumbria between 862 A.D. and 880 A.D. having been to revenge the death of Ragnar Lodbrog at the hands of Ella, king of the northern part of it, is not the only one accounting for the visits of these powerful hordes. Gaimar, a metrical chronicler connected with the family of Walter de Espec, the founder of Kirkham Priory and Rievaulx Abbey, and who wrote about the middle of the twelfth century, attributes the incursion of 867 A.D. to a very different cause, arising out of the gross sensuality and misconduct of Ella's rival, Osbert, king of such portions of Deira as Ella had not rent from him.

At this period Northumbria was in a state of civil war, and consequent lawless condition. The two kingdoms which constituted it were tearing each other to pieces. Ethelwulf, the bretwalder, and his immediate successors in that office, were too much occupied with defending and consolidating their more southern domains to interfere much with the internal strife of the north. Osbert or Osbrith was, at first, king of the whole of Northumbria. But proving a licentious tyrant, a successful rising among his subjects wrung from him Bernicia, and placed Ella, a knight of the province, upon the throne of that kingdom. Then followed years of internecine strife. Part, at least, of Northern Yorkshire seems to have been added by Ella to his domains at the expense of Osbrith. The latter, at last, fortified himself in York. Ella seems to have been marching from the north to attack him there, when the approach from the Eastern Counties, and up the Humber, of the common enemy, the Danes, led to a truce between them, and then to an agreement to unite their forces to resist the invaders.

This was the state of matters when the Danish leaders arrived in the Ouse, and halted to collect their forces at the town, probably Cawood, on its banks, where resided Buern the Busecarle. With this brief introduction the narrative of the chronicler will be better understood.

The commencement of the story is, of course, somewhat earlier.

Osbert, King of Northumbria, was staying at York. One day he went to hunt in the forest in the vale of York. There resided his baron, Buern the Busecarle, and at his house the king stayed to dine. The baron, however, at the time was absent at the sea, for because of outlaws he was deputed to guard it, but his wife—a most virtuous and beautiful lady—of whose beauty the king had heard report, was at home. When the king arrived he was received with every token of respect and honour, but he so terribly abused the hospitality of his vassal as to forcibly violate the lady. He then rode away to York.

'Buern,' says our chronicler, 'was a very noble and gentle man. Amidst all who frequented the sea, the land held not a better vassal; nor in the kingdom in which he was born was there a man better descended.' When on his return he saw his wife pale, and feeble, and thin, and found her so changed from what she was when he left, he asked what had occurred. She told him. A touching scene is then recorded, in which the husband's noble nature is conspicuous. At length he said, 'Since this felon committed this felony, I will demand that he shall lose his life.' In the morning the baron set out for York. He found the king among his nobles. Buern had many powerful relations there. The king saw him and called him. Then his vassal defied him, and said, 'I defy thee, and restore thee all; I will hold nothing of thee; never will I hold anything of thee; here I return to thee thy homage.' With this he went out of the house, and many noble barons accompanied him.

Then he held a council with his relations, and complained to them of the shame, and told all how the king had brought it upon him, and declared that he would go and, if possible, bring the Danes. His friends promised him that they would forsake and expel the king. And this they did so far as to drive him from the throne of Bernicia, and place Ella instead over that part of the kingdom. Osbert, however, held on to Deira, and fortifying himself against Ella in York, resisted all their efforts to expel him.

The arrival and reception by Buern of the Danes, and the result, shall be told in Gaimar's (Stephenson's translations) own words. They had wintered in East Anglia, the greater part of which they had subdued.

'In March, 867 A.D., they mounted themselves upon the best horses which had belonged to their vassals; and several of them went in ships as far as the Humber; they raised their sails; more than twenty thousand went there on foot. These Danes then turned, and passed the Humber at Grimsby with those on foot at the same time; they had great plenty of people. Those who were with the ships all went to York; both by water and land they waged great war at York.

'Those who had gone by water then sailed as far as the Ouse. But directly the sun was hidden the ebb tide returned; they then lodged themselves, some on the water, some in quarters.

'But the knights and barons went to the houses in the town. The nobleman whose name was Buern Busecarle lived there. He lodged all the lords very handsomely with great honour. He had assembled them thus and brought them from Denmark because of the shame of his wife, which he anxiously wished to avenge.'

'Those persons were lodged at Cawood who were in charge of the ships, but many of the Danes came by way of Holderness; they had spoiled the country till they came near the city; the ships also came against it. The king who then held the country was, upon the day on which they came upon the city, gone into the woods. But the other king was nigh, and he was deprived of the keys. When the Danes assailed them they defended themselves a little, but their defence was short, for the Danes gained the battle. Then the city was quickly taken, and there were a great many people slain. Osbrith, the king, was slain there. Buern, his enemy, was avenged.'

Death of Ella, King of Bernicia, near York.

At the taking of York, at the death of Osbert, Ella of Bernicia, his late rival, but now ally against the Danes, was absent from the city on a hunting expedition. The chronicler, as translated by the Rev. Joseph Stephenson, in the 'Church Historians of England,' shall again tell his own story of the event:

'Ella was in a forest; he had there taken four bisons. He was seated at dinner; he heard a man sound a bell; he held a little bell in his hand; it sounded as clear as a clock. The king begged before he came that he might have something to eat, for he asked for it. As the king was sitting at his repast, he said to a knight, "We have done well to-day; we have taken all we have hunted—four bisons and six kids; many times we have hunted worse." The blind man, who sat at a distance, heard him; then he said a word which was true: "If you have taken so much in the wood, you have lost all this country; the Danes performed better exploits who have taken York, and who have killed many barons. Osbreth's enemies have slain him." The king replied, "How do you know it?" "My sense has shown it to me. As a sign, if you do not believe me, the son of thy sister, Orrum, whom you see there, is to be the first killed in the battle at York; there will be a great battle; if you believe me you will not go forward. And, nevertheless, it cannot be otherwise; a king must lose his head." The king replied, "Thou hast lied; thou shalt be put in confinement and be severely treated. If this should be untrue thou shalt lose thy life; sorcery has been thy companion." The blind man replied, "I submit to this; if this is not the truth, kill me." The king had him brought with him, and commanded him to be well guarded. He put his nephew in a very high tower, that he might be there, and after he had summoned a guard he promised that he would send for him. The people of the country assembled, and went with the king towards York; they met many of the wounded, and of the flying, who related all that the diviner had said; not in one word had he lied; and King Ella, with many great people, rode onwards furiously.

'But the king's nephew, whom he had left up in the tower, committed a great folly. He took two shields which he had found, and went to the window; then putting his arms into the shields, he thought to fly, but he came to the earth with a great shock, then fell. Nevertheless, he escaped unhurt; not the least was he the worse for it. He saw a horse, which he quickly took. A knight was near, holding the horse by the bridle; three javelins he had in his hand. Orrum was no coward; he on the instant seized the javelins, while he also took the horse, and, having mounted him, rode away quickly. The enemy was then near York, and he spurred the horse, so that he arrived before the troops had mustered. Within himself he determined, like a foolish man, to strike the first blow. Into the rank that advanced first he threw the javelin he held. It struck a knight, whose mouth it entered, and came out behind the neck: he could not stand on his feet; his body fell lifeless; it could not be otherwise. He was a pagan; he cared nothing for a priest.

'Orrum held another dart, which he lanced on the other side. He wounded a vile Dane; so well he threw he did not miss; entering his breast, it went to his heart; he struck him dead. But as he (Orrum) wished to turn back, an archer let fly a dart; it wounded him so under the breast that mortal tidings reached the heart. The spirit fled, the body fell, exactly as the blind man had foretold. King Ella, when he knew this, felt in his heart a grief which he had never felt before. He cried out with boldness, and pierced through two of the ranks; but he did this like one out of his wits; he was quite beside himself. The Danes were on all sides; Ella the king was slain. He was killed in the field; few of his companions escaped. The place at which he was mortally wounded is now called Elle-croft; there was a cross towards the west; it stood in the midst of England. The English call it Elle-cross. No Dane had any rest till all this country north of the Humber was conquered.'

ELLSWORTH AND ELLE-CROSS.

What forest was-the one in which, according to the foregoing story, Ella was hunting when he received the news of the defeat and death of Osbert, is an interesting question, and especially so when taken in connection with the name of Ellsworth, in the forest of Knaresboro. Mr. William Grainge has brought forward considerable evidence to show that this Ellsworth must have been a residence, or hunting-lodge, of King Ella.

To touch upon this question, and epitomize what Mr. Grainge has written upon the subject, may trench very closely upon the region of history rather than belong to that of legend or tradition; yet it may be pardoned in this connection.

In the Yorkshire Archæological and Topographical Society's journal, page 427, vol. iv., an extract is given from a MS. in the library of Corpus Christi College, Cambridge, which states that Earl Ernulph resided at York near the bridge there, and that his wife had a property of her own, to which she retired, when her husband was engaged in his business abroad, at Beckwida, which was eighteen miles from York; and that Ella or Elle, who had been raised to be king, had a residence which he had constructed and named Ellesward, which was about six miles further distant from York than Beckwida, and in the same direction.

Beckwida may be probably identified with Beckwith, near Harrogate, the distance fairly corresponding. While a few miles to the west of Beckwith, and so more distant from York, is, or was, a hamlet named in Doomsday Book 'Elsword - Clifton,' and until recent times known as Clifton Elsworth, and Clifton-Cum-Norwood alias Ellsworth. These places are in what would in the time of Ella be 'forest primeval.' If this Elsworth, Elsward, or Elswath, was the place at which Ella's hall stood, it may be taken for tolerably certain that the forest in which Ella was hunting, and had taken 'four bison and six kids,' was the wild district to the west of Harrogate, afterwards known as the Royal forest of Knaresboro, and the hall in which the royal repast was spread, when the blind man with his bell attracted the royal attention, was this residence of the king at Ellswarth. The whole circumstances of the king's hurried ride to York, as related by the chronicler, imply that he had some considerable distance to travel before reaching that city, before which he met his death, or was taken captive, and afterwards slain.

The chronicler's account of the place where the king was mortally wounded is, in this connection, somewhat remarkable, and might reward further investigation. 'The Danes were on all sides; Ella the king was slain. He was killed in the field, few of his companions escaped. The place at which he was mortally wounded is now (1140 A.D.) called Ellecroft; there was a cross towards the west: it stood in the midst of England; the English call it Ellecross.'

The Danes in Yorkshire and St. Alkelda of Middleham.

> 'Beneath the shade the Northmen came,
> Fixed on each vale a Runic name,
> Reared high their altar's rugged stone,
> And gave their gods the land they won.'

The Danes were heathen, and with them they brought their heathenish cruelties. Christians and Christian institutions were peculiarly obnoxious to them. Lingard says of them, speaking of the years immediately following 867 A.D., when they overran Yorkshire, 'They could conceive no greater pleasure than to feast their eyes with the flames of villages which they had plundered, and their ears with the groans of the captives expiring under the anguish of torture. Their route was marked by the mangled carcases of the nuns, the monks, and the priests whom they had massacred. From the banks of the Ouse to the river Tyne, the towns, churches, and monasteries were laid in ashes; and so complete was their destruction that succeeding generations could with difficulty trace the vestiges of their former existence' ('Anglo-Saxon Churches,' vol. ii., p. 220).

At this time, and thus, amongst other pious foundations, St. Cuthbert's monastery at Crayke, St. Cedd's at Lastingham, and St. Hilda's illustrious house at Whitby were wiped out, though two of them were afterwards rebuilt.

'It is probably,' says Barker, the historian of Wensleydale, 'to this time that the martyrdom of St. Alkelda, of Middleham, must be assigned.'

Of the history, life, and death of this person very little indeed, or nothing, is really known. The churches of Middleham and Giggleswick are dedicated to her, showing her to have been in repute at the period in which they were founded.

Tradition and legend say that she was the daughter of a Saxon nobleman, and was put to death at Middleham, on account of her Christian faithfulness, by strangulation, by the Danes. In the east window of the north aisle of the church at Middleham, her sufferings are said to have been pictured in the glass; but all that remained, a few years ago, was a small portion representing her being strangled by two females, by means of a napkin twisted round her neck.

'Possibly,' again says Barker, who is also responsible for the story which follows, 'the scene of her suffering was the site of the present church, or a little to the west of it, for it is certain that her remains repose somewhere in the edifice.'

A spring which rises not far off is named St. Alkelda's well. The water of this fountain was accounted beneficial for weak eyes. Certain fee-farm rents in Middleham are required to be paid upon St. Alkelda's tomb, and were regularly deposited on a stone table in the middle of the nave, as also were some annual doles of bread, until the stone was removed, within the memory of some persons recently living.

A Norman Army stopped near Northallerton by fear of St. Cuthbert.

In 1069 A.D., Robert Cumin, whom William the Conqueror had nominated to the Earldom of Northumbria, was put to death, with 700 of his followers, by his turbulent subjects in the city of Durham.

William sent an army to subdue the revolt, and avenge the death of his sycophant. 'When they were approaching the town of Northallerton,' writes Roger of Howden, 'so great a darkness arose that one man could scarcely perceive his fellow, nor were they able, by any means, to discover which way to go.' While in this state of astonishment and bewilderment some person among them remarked that Durham, the city to which they were bound, had a powerful patron saint, St. Cuthbert, who was always an adversary to that city's adversaries, and none might molest it without incurring punishment from him. This soon spread through the army. Though rough soldiers, and inured to war and cruelty, they were not without superstition. They concluded the darkness was supernatural, and attributed it to the interference of the saint, and that rather than war against him, it would be more prudent to turn back to York, and there await the further instructions of William. And so they did. William had little fear of God, and less of St. Cuthbert, and, shortly afterwards, came down in person and exacted a fearful vengeance on these northern parts, which, alas! is matter of sad history rather than of tradition or legend.

II.

LEGENDS AND TRADITIONS OF ABBEYS AND OF MONASTIC LIFE.

Whitby Abbey.

'Whitby's nuns exulting told,
How to their house three barons bold
   Must menial service do;
While horns blow out a note of shame,
And monks cry, "Fye upon your name!
In wrath for loss of sylvan game,
   St. Hilda's priest ye slew."
This on Ascension Day each year,
While labouring on our harbour pier,
Must Herbert, Bruce, and Percy hear.
They told, how in their convent cell
A Saxon princess once did dwell,
   The lovely Edelfled;
And how, of thousand snakes, each one
Was changed into a coil of stone
   When holy Hilda prayed;
Themselves within their holy ground,
Their stony folds had often found.
They told how sea-fowl's pinions fail,
As over Whitby's towers they sail,
And sinking down, with flutterings faint,
They do their homage to the saint.'—Scott.

Thus lightly with his magic wand has the great Wizard of the North touched Whitby and its legends. When in the year 655 A.D. Oswy, the Christian King of Northumbria, was about to meet in battle Penda, the heathen tyrant of Mercia, he vowed, so say the chroniclers, that if he came off victorious he would dedicate his then infant daughter to a monastic life, and give twelve estates, or farms, to found religious houses. The battle, Winwaedfield, was fought, and Oswy was completely victorious. In fulfilment ot his vow, he committed his daughter, Ethelfleda, to the care and training of Hilda, and, having founded the abbey at Whitby, he translated her thither as its first abbess. Ethelfleda accompanied her, and ultimately succeeded her as head of the house.

The fame of Whitby — then Streoneshealh, 'the Bay of the Lighthouse'—under Hilda is matter of history.

We are concerned only with legend and tradition.

ST. HILDA'S WORMS.

When St. Hilda and her companions took possession of the new abbey, they were sorely troubled with a large number of snakes which infested its vicinity. Hilda prayed that they might all be driven over the sea-cliffs, and never return. She seconded her prayers by a vigorous onslaught upon them with a whip. They fled before her, and, in the haste with which they fled, they precipitated themselves over the rocks. By the fall their heads were broken off, or, according to another version, were cut off by the whip of the saint, and their bodies, coiling up, became instantly petrified and in this state some of them are still to be found upon the sands, and are known as Hilda's worms.

THE OBEISANCE OF BIRDS.

So great was the sanctity of the house of St. Hilda that the sea-fowls and other birds flying over it might never pollute it, but were compelled by instinct, or some other marvellous influence, to drop in their flight, and thus do lowly obeisance to its hallowed precincts. The wild goose, however, in its wildest career, would never fly over the place. So Drayton writes:

> 'Over this attractive earth there may no wild goose fly,
> But presently they fall from off their wings to earth;
> If this no wonder be, where's there a wonder found?'

CÆDMON THE POET.

In the days when holy Hilda ruled the abbey, there lived in the vicinity—probably a dependent upon the house—a cowherd named Cædmon. After the labours of the day were ended, he and his companions frequently met to enjoy themselves over a horn of beer. Music was an art cultivated among all classes in Saxon days, and more especially in the neighbourhood of the monasteries; and it appears to have been the custom, at such convivial meetings as those of Cædmon and his friends, to pass round the harp to each member of the company, and each was expected to sing a song to its accompaniment, for the entertainment of the rest.

This was a great trial to Cædmon, who was unable

to sing, and on such occasions he was accustomed furtively to slip from the room before his turn came to sing, and in solitude to mourn his hard fate.

On one occasion when this occurred he withdrew to the shed where his oxen were kept, and there, in the midst of his charge, fell asleep. During his sleep a vision appeared to him. There stood a man by him, who, calling him by his name, said, 'Cædmon, sing to me something.' 'Nothing,' said the cowherd, 'can I sing; and therefore it is that I have left the company and come hither.' 'Yet you must sing to me,' continued the man. Then 'What shall I sing?' asked Cædmon. 'Sing of the origin of things,' was the reply. At once he began to do so, and in verse he sang the praise of the Creator.

When the morning came and he awoke, he remembered the vision and all the words he had sung, and to them he added many others. He repeated them to his master, the reeve of the town, who at once took him to the abbey, and told the story, and revealed the great gift of song he had received to Hilda, the holy abbess.

She assembled the learned members and the disciples of her community, and bade Cædmon tell the vision and sing his verses in their presence. This he did. They all declared his power a heaven-bestowed gift. He was taken into the brotherhood; scripture narratives and histories were taught him, and he quickly turned them into the sweet melody of Anglo-Saxon song.

Thus originated Cædmon's poems, to which Milton owed much, and which stand first, in time, on the noble roll of English poetry.

Cædmon's death was in keeping with his inspiration

and life. The story of it has been thus told by a local writer:

'All that Cædmon wrote was to the intent of glorifying God and benefiting man; "for," says Bede, "he was a very pious man, and to regular discipline humbly subjected;" and his death was worthy of his life. Although apparently still far from his departure, being able to talk and walk about, he bade his servant prepare a place for him in the hospital of the monastery. This done, he repaired thither, and conversed cheerfully, and jested pleasantly, with some he found there. Midnight passed; then he called for the Eucharist. But as he looked little like dying, the attendants answered, "What need is to thee of the Eucharist? Thy departure is not so near, seeing now thou thus cheerfully and thus gladly art speaking with us." "Nevertheless," said he, "bring me the Eucharist." They brought it. Whereupon he, taking it in his hands, asked "if they had any ill-will toward him?" They all said "they were very kindly disposed to him," and they, in turn, besought him that he should be kindly disposed toward them all. Then he replied, " My beloved brethren, I am very kindly disposed to you, and to all God's men." Shortly he asked "how near it was to the hour that the brethren must rise and sing the nocturns?" They answered, "It is not far to that." He said, "It is well; let us wait the hour." Then he prayed, and signed himself with Christ's Cross, and reclined his head on the pillow, and slept for a little space; and then, in calm and stillness, passed away.'

This took place about the year 680 A.D.

THE HERMIT OF ESKDALE—A BROTHER OF WHITBY.

In the twelfth century—so says the story—a monk of Whitby retired to a hermit's cell, where was also a small chapel, dependent upon the abbey, in the woods of Eskdale-side. On Ascension Day, in the year 1140, three neighbouring nobles—William de Bruce, of Ugbarnby; William de Percy, of Snayton; and a Herbert or Allotson—met in these woods to hunt. A large wild boar, being hard pressed by his pursuers, took refuge in the chapel of the hermitage, and there, stretching himself out, died of exhaustion. The hermit immediately on his entry closed the door. The hounds stood baying before it. The hunters arrived, and demanded admission. The hermit complied, and opened the door; and there before them laid the prey, dead. In a moment of disappointment and anger, they rushed upon the hermit with their boar-staves, and mortally wounded him. Afraid at what they had done, they fled to Scarborough for sanctuary. Their crime not being privileged, they were surrendered at the demand of the Abbot of Whitby, and so stood in danger of the full penalty—that of death. The wounded hermit, however, while lingering at the point of death, desired his abbot to send for the offenders.

They were brought into his presence. 'I am sure to die of these wounds,' said the sufferer. 'Yes,' responded the abbot, 'and these shall also die for their crime.' 'Not so,' responded the dying man, 'for I freely forgive them my death if they are content to submit to this penalty for the good of their souls.'

They readily promised to do whatever he imposed upon them.

He then addressed them thus: 'You and yours shall hold your lands of the Abbot of Whitby and his successors on these terms. On the eve of Ascension Day you shall come to the woods of Eskdale-side; also at sunrise on the morrow (Ascension Day), the officer of the abbot shall blow his horn that ye may resort unto him. He shall deliver unto you, William de Bruce, ten stakes, eleven stowers, and eleven yadders, to be cut with a knife of a penny value; and to you, William de Percy, shall be assigned one-and-twenty of each sort, to be cut in like manner; and to you, Allotson, nine of each sort, also to be cut in like manner. These you shall take upon your backs and so carry them to the town of Whitby, and be there before 9 o'clock on the same morning. Each of you shall there set your stakes at low water at the brim of the sea. Each stake shall be a yard apart, and ye shall so "yadder" (tether?) them with your yadders, and stake them on each side with your stowers, that they shall stand three tides without being removed by the force of the waves. This ye shall do at the same hour on this day, every year, to remember you that you did slay me, and that you may repent you and do good works. The abbot's officer of Eskdale-side shall, at the same time, blow "Out on ye; out on ye; out on ye!" for this great crime. If you, or your successors, refuse this service, your lands shall be forfeited to the abbot or his successors.'

This legend accounts for a ceremony, somewhat similar, still observed on the sands at Whitby. One or more poetical versions of it are extant.

WHITBY ABBEY BELLS.

The abbey was suppressed in 1539 A.D., and shortly afterwards dismantled. The bells were sold, and were to be conveyed by ship to London. They were duly placed on board, and, amid the lamentation of the people, the sails were unfurled and the anchor weighed. But, lo! the vessel refused to bear away its sacred burden. A short distance it moved out into the bay, and then—on the beautiful, calm summer evening—it quietly sank beneath the waves; and there under the waters, at a spot within sight of the abbey ruins, the bells still remain, and are still heard occasionally, by the superstitious, rung by invisible hands. The legend is the subject of a beautiful poem by Mrs. Phillips, who sings :

> ' Up from the heart of ocean
>   The mellow music peals,
> Where the sunlight makes its golden path,
>   And the sea-mew flits and wheels.

> ' For many a chequered century,
>   Untired by flying time,
> The bells no human fingers touch
>   Have rung their hidden chime.'

Fountains Abbey.

In the year 1132 A.D., Richard, the Prior of St. Mary's Abbey at York, with twelve of his brethren of that house, partly separated themselves, and partly may be said to have been expelled, from the brotherhood, on account of their preferring a stricter rule than the Benedictine as administered by the somewhat easy-going Abbot of St. Mary's. They went forth, hardly knowing whither they went. Archbishop Thurstan took them, for a time, under his care and protection, and ultimately he determined to give them land, whereon to found a monastery, in the valley of the Skell. He had then a palace at Ripon, and, keeping Christmas there in 1132, he took the prior and monks with him, and together they selected the place, described then as 'a wilderness of rocks and trees,' in the valley near the hill called How Hill.

Here they were left in the depth of winter. There was no habitation near. Their only shelter was that afforded by seven yew trees, two or three of which are still remaining. In a short time they erected a hut round the trunk of a large elm-tree, their food being the bark of the adjoining elms, varied with leaves and herbs, and their drink water from the neighbouring springs.

Adopting the Cistercian rule, they were joined by one or two persons who brought a little property to the brotherhood, and things improved with them. A better habitation gradually arose.

While, however, they were still subject to privations, a traveller one day knocked at the gate, and asked for food.

'I have none to give you,' said the porter. But the man seemed weary and hungry, and as he persisted in begging, in the name of the blessed Saviour, for a loaf of bread, the porter went to the abbot, and inquired what he was to do.

'How much bread is there in the house?' asked the abbot.

'There are but two loaves and a half, and these are

wanted for the carpenters and others when they have finished their day's work.'

'Give the poor man one loaf,' replied the abbot; 'there will still be one and a half for the workers; as for us, God will provide as He sees best.'

This was done. But the straits to which the brotherhood was put had become known in the vicinity, and scarcely had this charity been bestowed, when, lo! there came to the gate of the convent two men with a cartload of bread, sent as a present for their relief by Eustace FitzHugh, the lord of Knaresborough Castle.

Better times followed, and Fountains became the mother of many monastic brotherhoods, and one of the first abbeys for wealth, grandeur and influence in the north.

RIEVAULX ABBEY AND KIRKHAM PRIORY.

WALTER DE ESPEC.

' And who's yon chiefe of giante heighte,
 And of bulk so huge to see?'
' Walter Espec is that chiefe's name,
 And a potente chiefe is hee.

' Hys stature's large as the mountaine oake,
 And eke as stronge hys mighte;
There's ne'ere a chiefe in alle the Northe
 Can dare with hym to fighte.'

Early in the twelfth century lived Walter de Espec, one of the foremost of the great barons of England, lord of Helmsley, Kirkham, and of many a fair manor besides.

By his wife, the Lady Adeline de Espec, he had an only son—the hope of his house—a fine, manly young

Yorkshireman, fond of the chase and a horse—a very Nimrod in the one, and a Jehu with the other. He bore his father's name of Walter.

One morning, about the year 1120 A.D., the Lady Adeline had a strange presentiment of danger at hand to her son. She earnestly endeavoured to induce him to forego his hunting for that day, and remain with her at home—but in vain.

In the evening, when the chase was over, a wayfaring man saw the young Lord of Kirkham riding at a furious pace towards the adjoining village of Firby. Suddenly, as he was passing a place where a spring of water gushed from a hill-side, and near which stood a wayside cross, a wild boar darted across the road in front of the rider. The horse swerved, and, stumbling, threw the youth from his seat. His head struck the stone at the foot of the cross, but one of his feet remained fixed in the stirrup. The horse, starting again, dragged him until the foot became detached from the stirrup, and, at a short distance from where he fell, young Walter de Espec was taken up dead.

The baron heard the sad news as one 'the desire of whose eyes had been taken away at a stroke.' He sought consolation and direction from his brother, who was rector of Garton, and by his advice he determined that a large portion of his estates should be devoted to the service of Him who had given and had taken away —that Christ and His poor should be his heir. Acting upon this resolution, Walter de Espec founded the Priory of Kirkham in 1122 A.D., the Abbey of Rievaulx in 1131 A.D., and that of Warden, in Bedfordshire, in 1136 A.D.

Kirkham Priory—the ruins of which by the Derwent form a beautiful object, of double interest, when he knows their origin, to the traveller by railway between York and Malton—arose on the spot where young De Espec met his death. The stone that forms the socket of a broken cross, before the gate-house now remaining, is the very one (so says our tradition) against which the youth was hurled; while the once high altar of the church of the priory stood on the place where the lifeless body was taken up.

WALTER DE ESPEC AT THE BATTLE OF THE STANDARD.

In 1138 A.D., nobly bearing his sorrow, Walter de Espec held high command in the English army at the battle of the Standard, or, as the old writers call it, 'Cuton Moor,' near Northallerton. A monk of Rievaulx thus describes him at that time: 'A man of stature passing tall, but of limbs well proportioned, and well fitted to his great height. He had his hair still black, though he was old and full of days; his beard was long and flowing, his forehead wide and noble; his eyes large and piercing; his face broad, but well featured; and his voice like the sound of a trumpet, setting off the natural eloquence of his speech with a kind of majesty of sound.' When De Espec had addressed the army, and encouraged them not to fear the greater number of the Scots, he took the hand of the Earl of Albemarle, the English commander, and said, 'I swear on this day to conquer or die on the field.' 'So swear we all,' said the barons; and then the fight began.

They conquered, and De Espec survived the battle some fifteen years. But two years before his death he retired from the world, and became a monk in the abbey, which he had founded at Rievaulx, and here, in 1153, he died and was buried.

These legendary and traditional incidents were seized upon by the late Archdeacon Churton, and woven into the following portion of his pretty ballad, 'Walter Espec.'

> 'Such life was Baron Walter's,
>   That chief of old renown;
> Lord of the woods of Galtres,
>   And Cleveland's mountains brown.
>
> 'One day he had of glory,
>   One day to memory dear,
> That long in England's story
>   The listening world shall hear;
>
> 'When he stood midst dead and dying
>   On Allerton's broad plain;
> Where the bolts from arblasts flying
>   Drank the blood of Scotland's slain;
>
> 'When with eye that never wandered,
>   And with heart that could not yield,
> Fast by the noble standard,
>   He kept the stubborn field;
>
> 'And his voice amidst the battle
>   Was heard at every stound,
> Above the din and rattle,
>   Like the silver trumpet's sound.
>
> 'But tell me why that old man
>   Endured that summer's day,
> When many a young and bold man
>   Was fain to quit the fray?

'What strong resolve had bound him
    To conquer or to die,
While each hardy knight around him
    Caught a courage from his eye?

'That ancient Baron Walter,
    His earthly hope was gone,
When he reared the solemn altar,
    Beneath the vault of stone.

'Where the silver Derwent wanders,
    By woods and meadows green,
Where the pitying muse still ponders,
    On things that once have been;

'He had rear'd the solemn altar,
    Beneath the vault of stone,
Resign'd, though his voice might falter,
    For he mourned his only son.

   .   .   .   .   .

'A courage more than mortal's
    That day had nerved his hand;
Angels from heaven's high portals
    Would guard his native land.

   .   .   .   .   .

''Twas done; ere curfew sounded,
    The battle-field was red,
And the northern host, confounded,
    Left twice five thousand dead.

   .   .   .   .   .

'Where the Rie its waves of amber
    Rolls o'er its bed of stone,
Where the wild deer stray or clamber
    The gray rocks all alone;

'There an abbey stands—more fair one
  No northern vale hath seen;
That abbey reared the baron,
  Those echoing hills between.

'There dwelt the monks, the wan ones,
  Who labour, fast, and pray,
Good Bernard's meek companions,
  In their cowls and frocks of gray.

'While the moon is on the mountains,
  And the moonlit air is still;
No sound, save of the fountains,
  Or the gushing near the mill.

'Now the midnight chant is ended,
  And the aisles are dark in shade,
And in chambers long-extended
  The convent sons are laid;

'Gaze softly, where the grating
  Gives to view the bed of heath,
There the baron rests, awaiting
  The welcome call of death.'

A PRIOR OF KIRKHAM'S HORSE.

A story told by St. Bernard, in the life of Malachy, Archbishop of Armagh, has a connection with Kirkham, and may be allowed here a place. It is one of a class of legends which would excite only ridicule and contempt, were it not that men such as St. Bernard, of the highest intellect of their days, have solemnly related them, and probably believed what they have told.

In the city of York there came to wait upon the Archbishop of Armagh a man of noble parentage,

William, Prior of the Brothers Regular at Kirkham, who, seeing that the archbishop had many in his company, and but few horses to carry them, offered him his own, only adding that he 'was sorry that it had been bred a draught-horse, and that its paces were somewhat rough. I would gladly offer you a better,' said he, ' if I had one, but if you will be contented to take the best I have, it may go with you.' 'I accept it most willingly,' said the prelate, ' because you say that it is worth little.' Turning then to his attendants, he said, ' Saddle me the horse, for it is a seasonable present, and it is likely to serve me long.' When saddled, he mounted it, and though at first he found its pace rough, after a little time, by a marvellous change, the motion became pleasant, and as gentle an amble as he could desire. And that no word that he had spoken might fall to the ground, the same animal never failed him for more than eight years. And what made the miracle more apparent was, that from iron-gray the horse began to grow white, so that not long after you could not find a horse more perfectly white than this had become.

THE ABBEY OF MEAUX OR MELSA.

Among the monks of Fountains, in the middle of the twelfth century, there was a certain Adam de Fountains, skilled in the architecture of the period, and with a strong passion for what we, in our degenerate days, should call 'bricks and mortar.' William le Gros, Earl of Albemarle, employed him in the erection of Vaudrey Abbey, in Lincolnshire. This nobleman happened one day to remark to his architect, that once he had vowed to make a pilgrimage to the Holy City, but his obesity, and his now increasing age, had prevented him from performing it. Adam promptly suggested that if he would build another Cistercian monastery it would do quite as well, for the fulfilment of his vow, as a tedious journey to Jerusalem. This the earl at once undertook to do.

The selection of the site upon his extensive estates was left to the monk. After journeying through them, about four miles east of Beverley, and seven or eight miles north of Hull, he came upon a delightful spot, ' embosomed in aged woods, adorned by native pools, and surrounded by fertile fields.' In the midst of the charming landscape arose a mound, or hill, called Mount St. Mary. Here, at the time of the Conquest, had settled a Norman follower of that monarch, named Gamel de Meaux, from his native place in France; and to this, his new home, the same name, Meaux, had been given. At this place, before the Mount St. Mary, the monk stopped, and fixing his staff in the earth, he exclaimed: 'This is the place that shall be called the vineyard of heaven and the gate of life! Have ye not heard, my brethren, what the prophet foretold concerning the building of the house of the Lord?—" In the last days the mount of the Lord's house shall be prepared on the top of a hill." These words I have been revolving all this day in my mind, and now I find that, by the especial appointment of Providence, a house of the Lord is to be erected on this very mount.'

The earl, his patron, had fixed previously upon the spot for a deer-park, and for that object had already begun its enclosure; he therefore raised this, as an objection, to Adam's selection of it for the monastery. The monk, however, urged the impossibility of altering what the will of heaven had declared, and he prevailed.

The spot was given for the monastery, and Adam revelled in the full scope given for his building talents; and the 28th of December, 1150 A.D., twelve monks of Fountains, with Adam at their head, left that abbey to take possession of the new monastery at Meaux. To its original name he, its first abbot, added another, that of Melsa, saying that for the delights of religion which would be practised in it, or, according to another account, from the sweetness and beauty of the spot itself, it might be compared unto heaven.

There is a *Chronicle of Meaux*, supposed to have been written by Thomas de Burton, 19th abbot, and brought down to 1406 A.D., which contains many curious records and legends. These relate chiefly to other parts of the country, rather than to Yorkshire. The following legendary scraps, however, may be of interest: 'A certain Jew of Tewkesbury fell into a cesspool on his Sabbath day, and would not allow himself to be taken out, in honour to the Sabbath. For a similar reason Richard de Clare, the lord of the town, would not permit him to be dragged out on the following day, being Sunday, out of reverence to his Sabbath; and so the Jew died in the pit into which he had fallen.'

Again, 'At the beginning of 1349 A.D., during Lent, six days before Easter Sunday, there occurred an earthquake throughout England so great that our monks of Melsa, while at vespers, on arriving at the verse in the evening canticle, "He hath put down the mighty from their seats," were by this earthquake thrown so violently from their stalls that they all lay prostrate on the ground.'

This chronicle has been published in three volumes in the series of chronicles, etc., issued under the direction of the Master of the Rolls.

BOLTON PRIORY.

Bolton on the Wharfe, with its ruined priory, 'which for picturesque effect has no equal among the northern houses, perhaps not in the kingdom,' seems to be the home of legend and tradition, as it has been the paradise of poets and painters. Turner delighted to paint its landscapes, and Landseer has depicted the riches of its parks, its granges, and its waters.

The priory and the legend of its foundation have provoked the efforts, from Wordsworth downwards, of poets and verse-writers, more than any other spot or subject in the county.

FOUNDATION OF THE PRIORY, AND THE BOY OF EGREMOND.

The legend, which from researches seems very legendary, of its foundation, in sober prose, is this. William de Meschines and his wife, the only daughter and heiress of William de Romille, a friend and partaker in the bounties of William the Conqueror, founded in 1220 A.D. a house for Augustinian monks at Embsay. Of their two daughters one, who inherited Craven, married William FitzDuncan, a nephew of David, King of Scotland. The only surviving child of this marriage, the one hope of his proud family, was a son, born at Egremond Castle, in Cumberland, and, from this place, popularly denominated 'the boy of Egremond.'

In the year 1251 A.D. the youth was on a hunting expedition in his mother's Craven domains, and, accompanied by his companion, came to the romantic spot on the Wharfe where, with terrible force, the waters of that river rush through a narrow cleft in the rocks, known, from the possibility of stepping across it, as the Strid. With a hound in leash, the boy of Egremond attempted this foolhardy feat. The hound suddenly hung back, and dragged backward his master into the seething channel, where, as many since his day have done the same, he perished. An affrighted forester hurried with the sad tidings to the Lady Adeliza, the youth's now doubly-widowed mother. She read the story in the dismay of his countenance. She learnt that she, the heiress of the De Romilles, was childless. She sought alleviation of her sorrow in works of piety. In pious memory of her son, she removed the house of her grandfather's foundation at Embsay to the nearest suitable spot to the fatal Strid. She increased considerably the endowments, and then, step by step, on the beautiful spot thus selected, arose in its grandeur and beauty what is now 'Bolton's mouldering priory.' The poet Rogers has treated the legend thus:

> 'Say what remains when hope is fled?
> She answered, "Endless weeping."
> For in the herdsman's eye she saw
> Who in his shroud was sleeping.
> At Embsay rang the matin bell,
> The stag was roused on Barden Fell;

> The mingled sounds were swelling, dying,
> And down the Wharfe a hern was flying;
> When near the cabin in the wood,
> In tartan clad and forest green,
> With hound in leash and hawk in hood,
> The boy of Egremond was seen.
> Blithe was his song, a song of yore;
> But where the rock is rent in two,
> And the river rushes through,
> His voice was heard no more.
> 'Twas but a step, the gulf he passed;
> But that step—it was his last!
> As through the mist he winged his way,
> (A cloud that hovers night and day),
> The hound hung back, and back he drew
> The master and his merlin too;
> That narrow place of noise and strife ;
> Received their little all of life.
> And now the matin bell is rung,
> The "Miserere" duly sung;
> And holy men in cowl and hood
> Are wand'ring up and down the wood,
> But what avail they?'

Wordsworth lays hold of the legend, and in his poem, 'The Force of Prayer,' deals with it more at length, and more in detail, though perhaps not more successfully than Rogers. The following portion contains his version of the principal incidents:

> '" What is good for a bootless bene?"
>   With these dark words begins my tale;
> And their meaning is, Whence can comfort spring
>   When prayer is of no avail?
>
> '" What is good for a bootless bene?"
>   The falconer to the lady said;

And she made answer, "Endless sorrow!"
    For she knew that her son was dead.

' She knew it by the falconer's words,
    And from the look of the falconer's eye;
And from the love which was in her soul
    For her youthful Romilly.

' Young Romilly through Barden woods
    Is ranging high and low;
And holds a greyhound in a leash,
    To let slip upon buck or doe.

The pair have reached that fearful chasm;
    How tempting to bestride!
For lordly Wharfe is there pent in
    With rocks on either side.

' This striding-place is called the Strid,
    A name which it took of yore;
A thousand years hath it borne that name,
    And shall a thousand more.

' And hither is young Romilly come,
    And what may now forbid
That he, perchance for the hundredth time,
    Shall bound across the Strid?

' He sprang in glee, for what cared he
    That the river was strong and the rocks were steep?
But the greyhound in the leash hung back,
    And checked him in his leap.

' The boy is in the arms of Wharfe,
    And strangled by a merciless force;
And never more was young Romilly seen
    Till he rose a lifeless corse.

    .   .   .   .   .   .

> 'Long, long in darkness did she sit,
>   And her first words were, "Let there be
> In Bolton, on the field of Wharfe,
>   A stately priory!"
>
> 'The stately priory was reared,
>   And the Wharfe, as he moved along,
> To matins joined a mournful voice,
>   Nor failed at evensong.'

. . . . . .

The number of minor and local poets who have versified the legend is almost legion, and it is somewhat invidious to make a selection from them. One poem, entitled 'The Boy of Egremond,' and published in Ingledew's 'Ballads of Yorkshire,' inscribed to John Bird, will be read with pleasure by those who can turn to it. Another, given by Dr. Dixon, alludes to the cruelties inflicted on the inhabitants of Craven by Fitz-Duncan, the father of the Boy of Egremond. Dr. Dixon states that it is transcribed from the album kept at the hotel at Bolton Bridge, and possesses at least one virtue—that of brevity. From its brevity and beauty combined it is subjoined:

'THE BOY OF EGREMOND.'

> 'She looked from the turret—the last beam of day
> Was tinting the mountains with golden array;
> The call of the herdsman came up from the dale—
> Alas!—'twas the only sound borne on the gale.
>
> 'She listen'd—all silent—the night-dew fell chill—
> No watch-dog bayed welcome—no bugle rang shrill;
> Why comes not the loved, the daring, the strong?
> Go! ask the wild torrent that murmurs along.

'In the homes of the valleys the childless ones weep;
Their morning how dreary—how broken their sleep;
Proud dame of the tyrant, weep with them and deem
If the sword hath its triumph, that so hath the stream.

'The gray monks of Embsay may pray for the dead,
And penance do duly, while mass right is said;
All bootless the bene is, and tear-drops will fall;
The voice that is silent earth cannot recall.'

THE WHITE DOE OF RYLSTONE.

Very closely connected with Bolton Priory is the legend of the White Doe of Rylstone. Whitaker, in his 'History of Craven,' gives the legend or tradition as follows:

'At this time' (*i.e.*, towards the end of the sixteenth century) 'a white doe, say the aged people of the neighbourhood, long continued to make a weekly pilgrimage from Rylstone over the fells to Bolton, and was constantly found in the abbey churchyard during divine service, after the close of which she returned home regularly, as the rest of the congregation. This incident awakens the fancy. Shall we say that the soul of one of the Nortons had taken up its abode in that animal, and was condemned to do penance for his transgressions against "the lords' deere" among their ashes? But for such a spirit the wild stag would have been a fitter vehicle. Was it not, then, some fair and injured female, whose name and history are forgotten? Had the milk-white doe performed her mysterious pilgrimage from Ettrick Forest to the precincts of Dryburgh, or Melrose, the elegant and ingenious editor of the "Border Minstrelsy" would have wrought it into a beautiful story.'

Wordsworth took up the challenge thus thrown down by the historian, and, weaving together this legend of the White Doe with the traditional account of the part played in 'The Rising in the North' by the Nortons of Rylstone, he gave to the world the poem of 'The White Doe of Rylstone; or, The Fate of the Nortons.'

Rylstone—the home of the Nortons—is some five or six miles over the fells from Bolton. The family, at the time to which the story related, consisted of the father, 'Old Richard Norton,' his nine sons, and their only sister, 'the gentle Emily.'

The rising in the North took place in 1569 A.D., at a time when the sufferings, from the dissolution of the monasteries, especially in these northern counties, were fresh on men's minds, and the hopes of the Romanists were turned to Mary of Scotland, as against the Protestant Elizabeth.

Percy, Earl of Northumberland, and Neville, Earl of Westmoreland, were at the head of the insurrection. A proclamation was issued that their object was to restore the ancient religion, to settle the succession, and to prevent the destruction of the old nobility. At Brancepeth they were joined by a large majority of the gentry, and their retainers, from the Yorkshire dales. Among the others came Richard Norton, with eight of his sons, bearing a banner embroidered with the five wounds of our Lord. The host entered Durham and desecrated the cathedral, and then advanced south as far as Clifford Moor, toward York, but changing their purpose, they turned back to lay siege to Barnard

Castle, held against them, for the queen, by Sir George Bowes.

The Earl of Sussex, President of the Council in the North, who lay with the royal forces in York, now ventured to follow the rebels. The leaders lost heart and retreated toward the Scottish Border, and then disbanded what followers remained to them, and thus left them to the vengeance of Sussex, while they found refuge in Scotland. Northumberland was, some years afterwards, betrayed by the Scots to the English, and beheaded. The Earl of Westmoreland died in exile in Flanders—the last of the Nevilles, Earls of Westmoreland. Richard Norton and his eight sons were (according to the tradition followed) taken at Barnard Castle, conveyed to York, and there put to death. Francis, the eldest son, who had refused to join the rising, was also slain, leaving the sister—Emily—as the only representative of the family.

This is, in outline, the traditional 'fate of the Nortons,' which, blended with the legend of the White Doe, becomes the subject of the poem.

The story as related by Wordsworth must, to be appreciated, be read as written by him; yet a *résumé* of his version of it can scarcely be omitted from 'Yorkshire Legends,' and may induce some to read, or re-read, the poem for themselves.

It opens with the gathering, on a Sunday morning, of the people from the hills and dales around Bolton to the service in the old church of the abbey—all that is spared of the once extensive pile. Few more attractive pictures have been drawn by poet's pen than this:

> 'From Bolton's old monastic tower
> The bells ring loud with gladsome power;
> The sun is bright, the fields are gay,
> With people in their best array,
> Of stole and doublet, hood and scarf,
> Along the banks of crystal Wharfe,
> Through the vale retired and lowly,
> Trooping to the summons holy.
> And, up among the moorlands, see
> What sprinklings of blithe company!
> Of lasses and of shepherd grooms,
> That down the steep hills force their way,
> Like cattle through the budded brooms;
> Path, or no path, what care they?
> And thus in joyous mood they hie,
> To Bolton's mouldering priory.'

The crowd of countryfolk first gathers in the churchyard and then passes into the church. And then is heard

> 'A hymn which they feel,
> For 'tis the sunrise now of zeal,
> And faith and hope are in their prime,
> In great Eliza's golden time.'

Then silence ensues as the minister proceeds to recite the other portions of the services:

> 'A moment ends the fervent din,
> And all is hushed, without, within.
>
> . . . . .
>
> The only voice which you can hear
> Is the river murmuring near.
> When soft!—the dusky trees between,
> And down the path through the open green,
>
> . . . . .
>
> And right across the verdant sod,
> Towards the very house of God,

> Comes gliding in with lovely gleam,
> Comes gliding in serene and slow,
> Soft and silent as a dream,
> A solitary Doe!
> White she is as lily of June,
> And beauteous as the silver moon.'

Again the voice of praise is heard within the sacred house, and, the service over,

> 'From the temple forth they throng,
> And quickly spread themselves abroad,
> While each pursues his several road.'

A knot, however, of the departing congregation gathers at a short distance from the spot where the White Doe has taken up her accustomed place, and

> 'Her Sabbath couch has made.'

These start amongst themselves various inquiries and surmises as to what can be the meaning of the weekly visits of this solitary animal to the churchyard. First a mother points her out to her boy—

> 'Look, there she is, my child; draw near,
> She fears not, wherefore should you fear?
> She means no harm.'

He, however, shrinks back and asks:

> 'But is she truly what she seems?'

Then an aged man, who has often been a partaker in the charity of the departed brotherhood, and has heard cld tales by the convent fire, expounds the legend of the Abbey's foundation, and expresses his opinion that the mysterious doe is no less than the troubled spirit of the Lady Adeliza haunting the spot of her now desecrated house. Next 'a dame of haughty air' thinks the doe has something to do with the murdered

Earl of Pembroke, or with his murderer, John de Clapham, for oft she loiters near

> 'A vault where the bodies are buried upright;
> There face to face and hand to hand
> The Claphams and Mauliverers stand;
> And, in his place, among son and sire,
> Is John de Clapham, that fierce esquire—
> A valiant man, a man of dread,
> In the ruthless wars of the White and Red—
> Who dragged Earl Pembroke from Banbury Church,
> And smote off his head on the stones of the porch.'

Finally

> 'A slender youth, a scholar pale,
> From Oxford come to his native dale,'

hath his own conceit with regard to the doe. To him she is the gracious sprite, or fairy, who attended upon the shepherd Lord Clifford, in his wanderings in early life in Cumberland, and his home at Barden,

> 'And taught him signs and showed him sights
> In Craven's dens and Cumbria's heights.'

The knot of listeners who have gathered round, now, still in uncertainty, disperse,

> 'And all the assembly own a law
> Of orderly respect and awe;
> But see—they vanish one by one,
> And last, the doe herself is gone.'

Having thus recorded these questionings and surmisings of the neighbours, the poet next proceeds to enter upon the real subject of his poem, and to give his story of the White Doe. For the purpose of this story, he goes back to the time immediately preceding the rising in the North, when the Nortons—father, sons, and the gentle Emily—were dwelling together in the beloved ancestral home at Rylstone. The banner of revolt, however, was already prepared, embroidered against her will, but at her father's request, by Emily.

> 'That banner, waiting for the call,
> Stood quietly still in Rylstone Hall.'

The call came, and the father and eight of his sons prepared to join the rebel earls. Francis, the eldest son, who, like his sister, had received the reformed faith from their now dead mother, refuses to take part in the expedition, and, with Emily, looks with despairing sorrow upon the enterprise. His object is misjudged, and he is accused of only wishing to save the lands from confiscation. One final effort he makes, before their departure, to persuade his father and brothers from it, and for this purpose throws himself at his father's feet, saying—

> ''Tis meet that I endure your scorn,
> I am your son, your eldest born;
> But not for lordship or for land,
> My father, do I clasp your knees.
> The banner touch not, stay your hand—
> This multitude of men disband,
> And live at home in blissful ease;
> For these my brethren's sake, for me,
> And, most of all, for Emily.'

The appeal is in vain. Norton, his sons, and retainers, depart, and Francis and his sister are left alone. He cannot, however, endure to remain inactive when his father and brothers may be in danger. Though he cannot join with them he follows them, that he may be at hand when the dreaded disaster comes, to serve them as best he may. Whatever of woe may befall them, he will share it with them. But before departing on this errand, he tries to prepare the lonely watcher, left at home, for the worst, and in a final interview he says:

> 'O sister, I could prophesy!
> The time is come that rings the knell
> Of all we loved, and loved so well;
>
> . . . . .
>
> Hope nothing, I repeat, for we
> Are doomed to perish utterly.
>
> . . . . .
>
> The blast will sweep us all away,
> One desolation—one decay!'

Then, observing a white doe, which, when a fawn, one of her younger brothers had brought to her as a present, and which had become the pet and companion of Emily, he added:

> 'Even this creature—
> Even she will to her peaceful woods
> Return, and to her murmuring floods,
> And be in heart and soul the same
> She was before she hither came—
> Ere she had learned to love us all,
> Herself beloved in Rylstone Hall.
> But thou, my sister, doomed to be
> The last leaf which, by heaven's decree,
> Must hang upon a blasted tree;
> If not in vain we've breathed the breath
> Together of a purer faith,
>
> . . . . .
>
> 'If we like combatants have fared,
> And for this issue been prepared—
> If thou art beautiful—and youth
> And thought endue thee with all truth—

> Be strong—be worthy of the grace
> Of God, and fill thy destined place—
> A soul, by force of sorrows, high
> Uplifted to the purest sky
> Of undisturbed humanity.'

In the next portion of the poem (Cantos iii. and iv.) there is a description of the assembling of the rebel forces at Brancepeth; of the unfurling of the Norton banner to be that of the whole army; an account of the sacrilege at Durham; and then of the march southward.

> ' Thence marching southward, smooth and free,
> They mustered their host at Wetherby,
> Full sixteen thousand fair to see;
> The choicest warriors of the North!
> But none for undisputed worth
> Like those eight sons; who in a ring,
> Each with a lance—erect and tall—
> A falchion, and a buckler small,
> Stood by their sire, on Clifford Moor,
> In youthful beauty flourishing,
> To guard the standard which they bore.'

Then comes vacillation and retreat, which brave old Norton strives hard to arrest. Francis Norton, who, unarmed, has followed every movement—

> ' Hath watched the banner from afar,
> As shepherds watch a lonely star '—

once more throws himself before his father, and beseeches him to withdraw from the ill-starred enterprise, but he is only spurned away by the veteran, and again retires to await the course of events. An already disorganized assembly, they lay siege to Barnard

Castle. A wild attack is made on the walls. The aged Norton, supported by his sons, dashes into a breach:

> ' The foe from numbers courage drew,
> And overpowered the gallant few,
> " A rescue for the standard !" cried
> The father from within the walls ;
> But see, the sacred standard falls !—
> Confusion through the camp spreads wide :
> Some fled—and some their fears detained ;
> But ere the moon had sunk to rest
> In her pale chambers of the west,
> Of that rash levy nought remained.'

The Nortons are all taken prisoners. Meanwhile Emily, with the white doe as her sole companion, is pining in her lonely watchings in Rylstone Hall. At last she sends out an old retainer to learn tidings of her absent ones. In due time he returns,

> ' That gray-haired man of gentle blood,
> Who with her father hath grown old
> In friendship, rival hunters they,
> And fellow-warriors in their day,
> To Rylstone he the tidings brought ;
> Then on this place the maid had sought :
> And told, as gently as could be,
> The end of that sad tragedy.'

' The end of that sad tragedy '—accepting the traditional account of the poet, which is in some respects not historically true—is, that her venerable father and his eight valiant sons were led to York in chains, and there condemned to death. Francis still hovered about them ; and getting access to their prison, received there the last command and blessing of his father. The banner—worked by Emily's own hand—was ordered to be carried, in mockery, before them to the place of execution. Francis, however, going up, claimed it as his property, and took it out of the hand of the soldier that bore it, and, unmolested, escaped with it through the crowd. His father's last command to him had been:

> ' " Hear then," said he, " while I impart,
> My son, the last wish of my heart.
> The banner strive thou to regain;
> And if the endeavour be not vain,
>
> . . . . .
>
> Bear it to Bolton Priory,
> And lay it on St. Mary's shrine—
> To wither in the sun and breeze
> 'Mid those decaying sanctities." '

Having heard this—the old retainer's sad, sad story—the stricken Emily awaits the coming of Francis, who is reported thus to have escaped. But—

> ' Why comes not Francis? thoughts of love
> Should bear him to his sister dear,
> With motion fleet as winged dove;
> Yea, like a heavenly messenger,
> An angel-guest, should he appear.'

Bearing the banner, which he had snatched from the mockery and degradation intended, he had hurried westward toward Bolton,

> ' And forward with a steady will
> He went, and traversed plain and hill,
> And up the vale of Wharfe, his way
> Pursued; and on the second day
> He reached a summit where his eyes

> Could see the towers of Bolton rise ;
> There Francis for a moment's space
> Made halt—but hark ! a noise behind
> Of horsemen at an eager pace !'

The execution of his father and brothers being over, the authorities at York then recollected how the banner had been taken from its guardian, and borne away by its captor. Sir George Bowes, with a company of horsemen, was hastily sent in pursuit. On the summit, whence he could see the towers of Bolton rise, the fugitive was overtaken, and, overpowered by numbers, he was slain.

The body of Francis lay two days on the wild moors. On the third day it was discovered by a forester belonging to the family. He, with others, bore it to Bolton Abbey for interment, hoping thereby to spare the gentle Emily the sight of a ghastly corpse. Unable to rest, however, under her anxiety, she wanders forth towards the ruined priory.

> 'She comes, and in the vale hath heard
> The funeral dirge ; she sees the knot
> Of people, sees them in one spot—
> And darting like a wounded bird,
> She reached the grave, and with her breast
> Upon the ground received the rest—
> The consummation, the whole ruth
> And sorrow of this final truth.'

Thus now left alone, the last of her ruined house, she assumes the dress of a pilgrim, and for several years wanders in places far and wide from Rylstone and Bolton.

At length she returns, and looks upon her childhood's home. Desolation and ruin have done their work at Rylstone Hall—and the very name of her family is almost forgotten. She, an unrecognised stranger, is found seated under an aged, blighted oak, the sole survivor of a luxuriant grove—

> 'When with a noise like distant thunder,
> A troop of deer come sweeping by;
> And, suddenly, behold a wonder!
> For, of that band of rushing deer,
> A single one in mid career
> Hath stopped, and fixed its large, full eye
> Upon the Lady Emily.
> A doe, most beautiful—clear white,
> A radiant creature, silver bright!'

It is her own white doe! Having for the long years of its mistress' wandering run wild with its fellows, it now recognises her, timidly advances, lays its head on her knees, and looks her in the face.

> 'The pleading look the lady viewed,
> And, by her gushing thoughts subdued,
> She melted into tears—
> A flood of tears that flowed apace
> Upon the happy creature's face.'

Henceforth the two become inseparable companions. Emily finds a home, or rather homes, among the humble peasantry of the neighbourhood, who had once been her father's tenants. Wandering from house to house among them, now

> 'A hut, by tufted trees defended,
> Where Rylstone brook with Wharfe is blended,'

and then

> 'Unwooed yet unforbidden
> The white doe followed up the vale,
> Up to another cottage hidden
> In the deep fork of Amerdale'—

she visits all the spots sacred to other days:

> 'But most to Bolton's sacred pile,
> On favouring nights she loved to go;
> There ranged through cloister, court, and aisle,
> Attended by the soft-paced doe.
> Nor did she fear in the still moonshine,
> To look upon St. Mary's shrine,
> Nor on the lonely turf that showed
> Where Francis slept in his last abode.'

At length death overtakes the lonely wanderer, and

> 'In Rylstone church her mortal frame
> Was buried by her mother's side.'

The faithful doe long survived its mistress; and it is during those years of its survival that, alone, it continues to frequent those haunts—Bolton Priory at the hour of service, and the grave of Francis Norton, where it and its gentle mistress had so often been found together—

> 'Haunting the spot with lonely cheer,
> Which her dear mistress once held dear;
> Loves most what Emily loved most—
> The enclosures of this churchyard ground,
> Here wanders like a gliding ghost,
> And every Sabbath here is found.'

Such is a mere outline of Wordsworth's version and rendering of the legend of the white doe, and the tradition of the fate of the Nortons. Legend and poetry are blended therein, with all the genius and skill of one of England's sweetest poets, to form one of the most delightful poems in the English language.

BARNOLDSWICK AND KIRKSTALL ABBEYS.

In 1147 A.D., that prolific mother of holy brotherhoods—Fountains Abbey—sent out twelve of its monks with ten of its lay brethren, under Alexander, its prior, to form the nucleus of a monastery, on a foundation which Henry de Lacy had laid for them, at Barnoldswick in Craven.

This nobleman, Lord of Pontefract, and of estates said to have extended for ninety miles in Yorkshire and Lancashire, was afflicted with a dangerous illness, during which he vowed that, should he recover, he would 'erect an abbey, for monks of the Cistercian Order, in honour of the most glorious Virgin and Mother of God, Mary.'

He recovered, and in performance of this, his vow, he had founded and endowed the House at Barnoldswick. But at this place the neighbours—many of whom had been removed from their homesteads to make room for the brotherhood—proved inhospitable as the climate. The monks liked neither. They complained that the situation was bleak, the lands barren, the seasons late and unfavourable for their crops, and, moreover, that it was very liable to the depredations of the Scots.

Alexander, the abbot, and his brethren were, therefore, on the look-out for more agreeable quarters.

The travels of the abbot, on the business of his house, brought him down the beautiful, fertile, and then smokeless valley of the Aire. Halting at one of its richest spots, sheltered by luxuriant woods, and with openings (*felds*) of rich meadowlands stretching out by the river-side, he espied the habitation of a small brotherhood of hermits. Seleth was the name of their leader, and he soon stood in the presence of the lordly Abbot of Barnoldswick. 'How came he and his fraternity,' demanded the abbot, ' to be in possession of this fertile spot ?' Then Seleth related that, at his distant home in the south, he had had in his sleep a vision, and had heard a voice saying, 'Arise, Seleth, and go into the province of York; and seek there for a valley called Airedale, and for a place called Kirkstall; there shalt thou provide a habitation for me and my son.' Enquiring, 'Who art 'thou ?' the person who appeared to him replied, 'I am Mary, and my son is Jesus of Nazareth.' Thus directed, Seleth related how he had arisen and journeyed into Yorkshire, and, after many vicissitudes and wanderings, had arrived in Airedale, and fixing upon this spot he had learned, from the shepherds around it, that it was named Kirkstall. He, therefore, had here erected his humble abode. For a long time he had dwelt alone, subsisting on roots and herbs, and the hospitality of the scattered inhabitants. Then a few others of like spirit to his own had joined him, and thus had formed the small community.

'During this reply,' says Whitaker, 'the Abbot of Barnoldswick sent his eyes around to contemplate the site and advantages of the place, the beauty of the valley, the river winding through it, the quarries of fine freestone upon the spot, and the timber trees in the adjoining woods.' He soon saw that this was a better place than Barnoldswick, and remembered too that their patron, De Lacy, was feudal lord of the fee. His mind was made up. William de Poictou was the immediate owner under De Lacy, but that need not stand in the way. The abbot hastened away to Pontefract, and explained to De Lacy all the disadvantages of Barnoldswick, and all the advantages of the place inhabited by the hermits, and called Kirkstall. The grant of the place was soon settled. Seleth and his companions were disposed of—some by a money payment, and some (of whom Seleth was one) by incorporation into the fraternity of the new owners. Barnoldswick was abandoned, and in place of the cell of Seleth the Hermit sprang up, by the munificence of De Lacy, and under the superintendence of Alexander, the first abbot, the beautiful and extensive Abbey of Kirkstall.

The late J. H. Dixon, LL.D., expressed, and extended to later times, the dream of Seleth, thus—

'The vision of Seleth! a dream of the night!
A fair river flowed through a valley of light;
Gay flower-spangled meadows were spread o'er the scene,
And the forest birds sang from the ash branches green.

'The vision of Seleth! a dream of the night!
That stream was as lovely, those heavens as bright;
But o'er the pure waters a tall abbey frowned,
And the white-vested bedesman was pacing around.

'A vision of Seleth! a dream of the night!
The lofty-arched chancel in sable was dight;

Low chanted the monks 'mid the death-bell's dread toll;
And they prayed for the abbot—they prayed for his soul!

'The vision of Seleth! a dream of the night!
On a desolate ruin the moonbeams shone bright;
Wild screamed the foul raven, and dark ivy twine
Clung close to the alder, that waved o'er the shrine.'

MARY, THE MAID OF THE INN.

Who does not remember Southey's exquisite and pathetic ballad, 'Mary, the Maid of the Inn'?—

'Whose cheerful address fill'd the guests with delight,
  As she welcom'd them there with a smile;
Whose heart was a stranger to childish affright,
  And who would walk by the abbey at night
When the wind whistled down the dark aisle.'

The incidents of the ballad are very difficult to fix to Kirkstall. The author averred that they were true, and actually occurred at one of the northern abbeys—*either Furness or Kirkstall*, he could not remember which. On this ground it has been claimed for Kirkstall, and until some other place has proved a better claim than this Yorkshire abbey, far be it from a Yorkshireman to refuse it a place among the poetic legends of the county.

Mary was the maid at an inn near the abbey:

'She loved—and young Richard had settled the day,
  And she hop'd to be happy for life;
But Richard was idle and worthless; and they
Who knew him would pity poor Mary, and say
  That she was too good for his wife.'

Two guests had arrived at the inn, and, sitting by the fire on the dark, stormy autumn night:

> '"'Tis pleasant," cried one, seated by the fire-side,
>   "To hear the wind whistle without."
>   "A fine night for the abbey," his comrade replied,
>   "Methinks a man's courage would now well be tried
>   Who would wander the ruins about.
>
> '"I, myself, like a schoolboy, should tremble to hear
>   The hoarse ivy shake over my head;
>   And could fancy I saw, half persuaded by fear,
>   Some ugly old abbot's grim spirit appear:
>   For this wind might awaken the dead."

The other replied, that he would lay the wager of a dinner that Mary would venture to the ruins and bring from thence

> 'A bough
> From the alder that grows in the aisle.'

. . . . . .

'With fearless good humour did Mary comply.'

The rest must be told in the poet's own words:

> 'O'er the path so well known proceeded the maid,
>   Where the abbey rose dim on the sight;
>   Through the gateway she entered—she felt not afraid,
>   Yet the ruins were lonely and wild, and the shade
>   Seem'd to deepen the gloom of the night.
>
> 'All around her was silent, save when the rude blast
>   Howl'd dismally round the old pile;
>   Over weed-covered fragments still fearless she pass'd,
>   And arrived at the innermost ruin at last,
>   Where the alder-tree grows in the aisle.

'Well pleased did she reach it, and quickly drew near
  To hastily gather a bough,
When the sound of a voice seemed to rise on her ear;
She paused, and she listen'd, all eager to hear,
  And her heart panted fearfully now.

'The wind blew, the hoarse ivy shook over her head,
  She listen'd—nought else could she hear;
The wind ceased, her heart sunk in her bosom with dread,
For she heard in the ruins distinctly the tread
  Of footsteps approaching her near.

'Behind a wide column, half breathless with fear,
  She crept to conceal herself there;
That instant the moon o'er a dark cloud shone clear,
And she saw in the moonlight two ruffians appear,
  And between them a corpse did they bear.

'Then Mary could feel her heart's blood curdle cold—
  Again the rough wind hurried by—
It blew off the hat of the one, and behold
Even close to the feet of poor Mary it roll'd;
  She fell, and expected to die.

'"Curse the hat!" he exclaims. "Nay, come on and first hide
  The dead body," his comrade replies;
She beheld them in safety pass on by her side;
She seizes the hat, fear her courage supplied,
  And fast through the abbey she flies.

'She ran with wild speed, and rushed in at the door,
  She gazed in her terror around;
Her limbs could support their faint burden no more;
But exhausted and breathless she sank on the floor,
  Unable to utter a sound.

'Ere her pale quivering lips could her story impart,
  For a moment the hat met her view;
Her eyes from the object convulsively start,
For, O God! what cold horror thrilled through her heart,
  When the name of her Richard she knew!

'Where the old abbey stands on the common hard by,
  His gibbet is now to be seen:
Not far from the inn it engages the eye.
The traveller beholds it, and thinks with a sigh,
  Of poor Mary, the maid of the inn.'

Origin of Selby Abbey.

About the time of the Norman conquest of England, there resided, in the monastery of Autun, in France, a monk who bore no good character for honesty among his brethren. To him St. Germanus (so he claimed) appeared in a vision, and warned him of some approaching danger to himself from his brother monks. By night, therefore, he fled from the convent, and took with him, as a precious relic and talisman, one of the most sacred possessions of the house—the finger of the saint (St. Germanus) who had appeared to him.

Many adventures befell the fugitive by sea and by land; but at length he found himself off the coast of Yorkshire. Passing up the Humber, he came to a place where was a river-bay, much frequented by seals, and (so says the chronicler) so called *Sealby*. Here he landed, and, under a large and spreading oak near the river-side, he erected a large cross, and deposited by it his treasured relic, and spent much time in devotion before them.

One day Hugh, the Norman sheriff of the county,

passing up the river, noticed the cross. He made inquiries as to the cause of its erection there, and, having heard the monk's story, on his departure, he left him his own tent, to be a tabernacle for so precious a relic as the glorious finger of St. Germanus.

From this beginning sprang the Abbey of Selby. The Conqueror himself, by his sheriff or otherwise, became greatly interested in it. In 1070 A.D. he visited the place, and gave lands for the site and endowment of the holy house. Wooden cells were first built, and then the extensive domestic edifices. The sheriff's tent was replaced by a worthy church, portions of which still form part of the Abbey Church. Thus the great abbey, dedicated to St. Mary and St. Germanus, arose, whose abbot, with the exception of the abbot of St. Mary's at York, was the only mitred abbot north of the Trent.

The Gray Palmer and Hylda, the Nun of Nun-Appleton.

Nun-Appleton, on the Wharfe, once the seat of the great Parliamentary General Thomas, third Lord Fairfax, and now of Sir F. Milner, was formerly the site of a somewhat important nunnery, dedicated to God and St. Mary, hence the first syllable of its name. At no great distance from this convent, and (so says tradition) connected with it by a subterranean passage, was an establishment for monks, at Acaster Malbis. Connected with these, the following legend is told:

'In the year 1281 A.D. the Lady Abbess of Nun-Appleton called the Archbishop of York from his castle at Cawood to chant High Mass on the eve of St.

Mark, in order to lay at rest the wandering spirit of Sister Hylda, which had haunted the convent and monastery and the adjacent country during seven long years.

'The peasants fled from the district, for the spirit appeared to them in their homes, glared at them in the fields, or floated over their heads in passing the Wharfe; and if they attempted to fell a tree in the woods, a hideous form, in a Cistercian habit, presented itself, showing a wound in its breast. Now and then the moving wind would raise the black veil of the mysterious visitor, and disclose a ghastly countenance and sunken eyes, the latter raining incessant tears.

'On the eve of the celebration of High Mass, a tempest, with loud, dismal, and portentous howlings, shook the high craggy cliffs above Otley. Fierce and wild it whirled along the river, and sent levin bolts, and showered red meteors, over the cloisters of Nun-Appleton. Rain descended as if the firmament of heaven were dissolved into rolling tides; and the Wharfe, swelling over its banks, washed rocks from their base, and lofty trees from their far-spreading roots.

'But now the holy archbishop, in sacred stole, was before the altar, the veiled sisters of the Virgin Mary stood by the choir; the monks of Acaster Malbis were arranged beyond the fretted pillars of the chapel, and waited the solemn call of the bell to raise their voices in hymns of supplication.

'Presently the walls resounded with knocking at the convent gate. The portress told her beads and crossed her breast, as she said to herself, while wending to the portal, "There come other pilgrims of Palestine, foretold by the dreary ghost of Sister Hylda."

'The lock turned with difficulty. It seemed to deny admission to the stranger, for the hinges resisted and creaked horribly against his ingress, but the arm of the portress forced them to expand, and the Palmer, clad in gray weeds of penitence, strode within the threshold.

'The roaring thunder burst over his head, blue lightning flashed around his gigantic figure, and, in a hoarse, sepulchral voice, he thanked the portress for her gentle courtesy.

'"By land and sea," said he, "I have proved all that is terrible in danger, or awful in the strife of war. My arm wielded the truncheon with gallant King Richard, the chiefest of the holy rood; and the Paynims of Acre, with their mighty Soldan, have quaked in the tumult of our Crusaders. The storm of the Red Sea, and the rage of open ocean, have rattled in mine ear. I have crossed burning sands, and met the wild lords of the desert in shocks of steel; but never was my soul so appalled as by the rage of the elements this horrible night. To the sinner naught is so fearful as the working of the Almighty's wrath in our lower world. I have visited every shrine of penitence and prayer, to purge the stains of crime from this labouring bosom. I have trodden each weary step to the Holy Sepulchre in Palestine. I have knelt to the saints of Spain, of Italy, and of France. I have mourned before the shrine of St. Patrick, and every saint of Ireland. In Scotland I have drunk of every miraculous fount and holy well; and, but for the swollen waters of the Wharfe, I had sought the gray towers of Cawood, or the fair Abbey of Selby, to crave prayers from the pure of heart for the worst of transgressors. At holy St. Thomas's tomb my pilgrimage ends; but for the wicked there can be no rest. The pelting hail-blast, the dark, red flashes of lightning, and the flooded Wharfe opposed my course. I wandered through the dark wood. Dire peals of thunder roared among the groaning oaks, and the ravening he-wolf rushed from his den across my path—the flame of his eyes showed his gore-dripping jaws, wide asunder to devour me. A spectre, more fell than the rage of a savage beast, drove it away. The croaking raven and ominous owlet rung a death warning, and the spectre shrieked in my ear—" Gray Palmer, thy bed of dark, chill, deep earth and thy pillow of worms are prepared—thy flesh-less bride waits to embrace thee."

'Deep sounded the bell.

'"Haste thee, haste thee, holy Palmer," said the portress, "for the spectre of Sister Hylda bade the Lady Abbess expect thee. Haste thee to join the choral swell. Why quakes thy stately form? Haste thee—the bell has ceased its solemn invocation."

'Scarcely had the Palmer entered the sanctified dome of the chapel, when the seven hallowed tapers, which burned with perpetual blaze before the altar, expired in blue hissing flashes. The full swelling choir sunk to awful silence. A gloomy light circled along the vaulted roof, and Sister Hylda, with her veil thrown back by her skeleton hand, revealed her well-known features, but pale, grim, and ghastly, with the hue of the tomb, as she stood by the Palmer, who was recognised as Friar John.

'The archbishop raised his meek eyes and blanched countenance to Him that liveth and reigneth for ever. The cold dew of horror dropped from his cheeks, but in aspirations of prayer his courage returned, and, in adjurations by the name of the Most High, he commanded the spectre to tell why she broke the peace of the faithful?

'Unearthly groans issued from her colourless lips; the dry bones of her wasted carcase rattled, with a fearful agitation, as thus she spoke:

'"In me behold Sister Hylda, dishonoured, ruined, murdered by Friar John in the deep penance vault! He stands by my side, and bends his head lower and lower in confession of his guilt. I died unconfessed, and seven years has my troubled and suffering spirit walked the earth, when all were hushed in peaceful sleep, but such as the lost Hylda. Your masses have earned grace for me. I now go to my long rest. Seek the middle pavement-stone of the vault for the mortal relics of a soul purified and pardoned by the blood of the Redeemer. Laud and blessing to His gracious name for ever."

'Soft strains of melody swelled in the air, and a bright flame rekindled the holy tapers, but Sister Hylda and the Palmer vanished, and were never seen more.'

ROCHE ABBEY.

The ruins of Roche Abbey stand in a most picturesque and beautiful valley, near Sandbeck Park, in South Yorkshire.

In the year 1147, Durandus, a monk of New Minster,

in Northumberland, accompanied by twelve brother monks, wandered away from their parent abbey in search of 'fields and pastures new.' In course of their wanderings they hit upon this beautiful spot. Upon a prominent part of the limestone rock they observed—partly, perhaps, the work of nature and partly the work of some pious inhabitant of the place—an image of the Saviour on the cross. This at once led to the decision that this was the place which Providence intended to be their new home. Here, therefore, they settled; and through the liberality of the neighbouring lords, soon their beautiful house arose, and became known as 'The House of the Monks of the Rock' (de Rupe); hence the name of Roche or Rock.

A very sweet poetical version of the legend has been made by a living poetess, Miss Lush, a few stanzas only of which may be quoted; but the whole ought to be read:

'To a valley green embowered,
 Sentinelled by limestone gray,
Just when Nature's hand had showered
 Prodigal her gifts of May,
Came a band of Pilgrim friars at the closing of the day.

'Sunset tints of rose were falling
 Every leaf and branch across;
Suddenly the strangers' calling
 Echoed loud as if in loss;
In the fractured crag before them lay Christ stretched upon the cross.

'As the sun in golden glory
 Shed a nimbus round the head,

And, so runs the monkish story,
    Hands and feet were tinged with red,
Slowly spake the holy figure: " Here ye raise My Church," it said.

'Softly then the vision faded,
    But its bidding was fulfilled ;
Maltby's lord the Brothers aided,
    Gave the land whereon to build.
So they raised a stately abbey as the Holy Christ had willed.

.   .   .   .   .

'Centuries have swiftly fleeted,
    Ruined is the sacred pile,
That erstwhile the vision greeted,
    Fretted canopy and aisle;
Only Nature in the valley looks up with her ancient smile.

.   .   .   .   .

'Now the only incense rising
    Is the incense of the flowers,
And the larks, the matins prizing,
    Sing them still in morning hours,
While a choral strain at vespers rings through all the leafy bowers.

.   .   .   .   .   .

LEGENDS CONNECTED WITH ST. JOHN OF BEVERLEY.

'Oh, come ye from the east, or come ye from the west,
    Or bring ye relics from over the sea ;
  Or come ye from the shrine of St. James the Divine,
    Or St. John of Beverley ?'

SCOTT.

It is scarcely within the province of a series of papers on legends and traditions to enter the region of authentic history, further than is necessary to give pegs on which to hang the legendary stories.

Of the life of St. John of Beverley, therefore, it must suffice to say that he was probably the scion of a noble Saxon family, and born at Harpham on the Wolds, about the middle of the seventh century. He was brought up in the school of the prophets of that period —the Abbey of Whitby, and was afterwards a disciple of Theodore of Tarsus, Archbishop of Canterbury. He was elected Bishop of Hexham in 688 A.D., and in 705 A.D. was translated to York, the bishopric of which he held until 717 A.D., when he retired, and spent the four remaining years of his life in the monastery which he had founded at Beverley. Here, too, he was buried, first in the porch of the monastery; but, after his canonization by Benedict IX., his remains were removed to the Minster or Abbey Church, where his shrine or tomb was for long the glory of Beverley.

There are many legendary stories given by Bede, Foulchard, and other old writers, of wonders performed during his life in the more northern parts of the country, but the following refer to Yorkshire.

A LEGEND OF WATTON NUNNERY.

Sometime after St. John came to the see of York, he paid a visit to the nunnery of Watton (Vetadum) in the East Riding. The abbess was at that time named Heriburg. 'When we were come thither,' says the old chronicler, Abbot of Beverley, 'and had been received with great joy by all, the abbess told us that one of the younger inmates, who was her daughter according to the flesh, laboured under a very grievous distemper, having been lately bled in the arm, and, whilst she was engaged in study, was seized with a sudden violent pain, which increased so that the wounded arm became worse, and so much swelled, that it could scarce be grasped with both hands; and thus being confined to her bed, through excess of pain, she seemed about to die very soon. The abbess entreated the bishop that he would vouchsafe to go in and give her his blessing; for that she believed she would be the better for his blessing, or if he touched her. He asked when the maiden had been bled? and being told that it was the fourth day of the moon, said, "You did very indiscreetly and unskilfully to bleed her on the fourth day of the moon; for I remember that Archbishop Theodore, of blessed memory, said, that bleeding at that time was very dangerous, when the light of the moon and the tide of the ocean is increasing; and what can I do to the girl if she is like to die?"

'But she still earnestly entreated for her daughter, whom she dearly loved, and designed to make abbess in her stead; and at last she prevailed with him to go in to her. He accordingly went in, taking me with him, to the virgin, who lay, as I said, in great anguish; and her arm was so much swollen that no power of bending remained in the elbow; the Bishop stood and said a prayer over her, and having given his blessing, went out. Afterwards, as we were sitting at table, at the usual hour, someone came in and called me out, saying, " Quoenburg " (that was the virgin's name) " desires you will immediately go back to her." I did so; and as I entered, I perceived her countenance more cheerful, and like one in perfect health. Having seated myself down by her, she said, " Would you like me to ask for something to drink?" "Yes," said I, "and am very glad if you can." When the cup was brought, and we had both drunk, she said, "As soon as the bishop had said the prayer, and given me his blessing, and had gone out, I immediately began to mend; and though I have not yet recovered my former strength, yet all the pain is quite gone from my arm, where it was most intense, and from all my body, as if the bishop had carried it away with him, though the swelling of the arm still seems to remain." When we departed from thence, the cure of the pain in her limbs was followed by the assuaging of the fearful swelling.'

PUCH, THE EARL, OF SOUTH BURTON.

The same writer relates another story:

'Not far distant from our monastery (Beverley), *i.e.*, about two miles off, was the country house of one Puch, an earl, whose wife had languished nearly forty days under an acute disease, insomuch that for three weeks she could not be carried out of her room. It happened that the man of God was, at that time, invited thither, by the same earl, to consecrate a church; and when the church was dedicated, the earl desired him to dine at his house. . . . . Having, after some delay, prevailed on him to do so, we went to dine. The bishop had sent, to the woman who lay sick, some holy water, which he had consecrated for the dedication of the church, by one of the brethren, ordering him to give her some to taste, and to wash the place where her greatest pain was with some of the water. This being done, the woman immediately got up in health, and perceiving that she had not only been delivered from her tedious disease, but at the same time had recovered the strength she had lost, she presented the cup to the bishop and to us, and continued to serve us with drink, as she had begun, until dinner was over.'

THE TWO SISTERS OF BEVERLEY.

One, if not two, of the daughters of this Puch, the earl, entered the convent at Beverley. According to Poulson, the historian of Beverley, there is in the south aisle of the Minster an altar tomb placed under a pinnacled canopy, and covered with a slab of Purbeck marble, but without any inscription or anything to lead to a knowledge of the occupant or occupants. Tradition, however, assigns it to the unmarried daughters of Earl Puch, who are said to have given two of the common pastures to the freemen of Beverley.

In Ingledew's 'Ballads of Yorkshire' there is a legendary ballad relating to the mysterious appearance, and disappearance, of these ladies at the convent. The first, on Christmas Eve, is described thus:

> ' The tapers are blazing, the mass is sung,
>   In the Chapel of Beverley,
> And merrily too the bells have rung;
>   'Tis the eve of our Lord's nativity;
> And the holy maids are kneeling round,
> While the moon shines bright on the hallow'd ground.

> 'Yes, the sky is clear, and the stars are bright,
>   And the air is hush'd and mild;
> Befitting well the holy night,
>   When o'er Judah's mountains wild,

> The mystic star blazed bright and free,
> And sweet rang the heavenly minstrelsy.
>
> 'The nuns have risen; through the cloister dim,
>   Each seeks her lonely cell,
> To pray alone till the morning hymn
>   On the midnight breeze shall swell;
> And all are gone save two sisters fair,
> Who stand in the moonlight silent there.
>
> 'Now hand in hand, through the shadowy aisle,
>   Like airy things they've past,
> With noiseless step, and with gentle smile,
>   And meek eyes heavenward cast;
> Like things too pure upon earth to stay,
> They have fled like a vision of light away.'

. . . . . .

On the eve of St. John's Day, early in the month of May, they again return:

> 'The snows have melted, the fields are green,
>   The cuckoo singeth aloud,
> The flowers are budding, the sunny sheen
>   Beams bright through the parted cloud,
> And maidens are gathering the sweet-breath'd may;
> But these sisters, oh, where are they?
>
> 'And summer is come in rosy pride,
>   'Tis the eve of the blessed St. John,
> And the holy nuns after vespertide,
>   All forth from the chapel are gone;
> While to taste the cool of the evening hour,
> The abbess hath sought the topmost bower.'

. . . . . .

From her place in the turret the abbess descries the two mysterious sisters asleep on the threshold of the convent door, and—

'Then again the chapel bell is rung,
  And all to the altar repair,
And sweetly the midnight lauds are sung,
  By the sainted sisters there ;
While their heaven-taught voices softly rise
Like an incense cloud to the silent skies.

'The maidens have risen, with noiseless tread
  They glide o'er the marble floor ;
They seek the abbess with bended head,—
  "Thy blessing we would implore,
Dear mother, for ere the coming day
Shall burst into light, we must hence away."

'The abbess hath lifted her gentle hands,
  And the words of peace hath said,
" *O vade in pacem,*"—aghast she stands !
  Have the innocent spirits fled ?
Yes, side by side, these maidens fair,
Like wreaths of snow in the moonlight there.

'List ! list ! the sweet peal of the convent bells,
  They are rung by no earthly hand,
And hark, how the far-off melody swells
  Of the joyful angel band,
Who hover around surpassingly bright,
And the chapel is bathed in a rosy light !

' 'Tis o'er ! side by side in the chapel fair
  Are the sainted maidens laid ;
With their snowy brow, and their glossy hair,
  They look not like the dead !
Fifty summers have come and passed away,
But their loveliness knoweth no decay !

'And many a chaplet of flowers is hung,
  And many a bead told there,

> And many a hymn of praise is sung,
> And many a low-breathed prayer;
> And many a pilgrim bends the knee,
> At the shrine of the sisters of Beverley.'

EARL ADDI'S SERVANT, OF NORTH BURTON.

It is, again, related by Bede that St. John of Beverley was, on another occasion, called to dedicate a church, built by Earl Addi, at North Burton. 'When he had performed that duty, he was entreated by the same earl to go in to one of his servants, who lay dangerously ill, and, having lost the use of all his limbs, seemed to be at the point of death; and, indeed, the coffin had been provided in which to bury him. The earl urged his entreaties with tears, earnestly requesting that he should go in and pray for him, because his life was of great consequence to him, and he believed that if the bishop would lay his hands upon him, and give him his blessing, he would amend. The bishop went in, and, seeing him in a dying condition, said the prayer with him; and on going out, said, "May you soon recover." Afterwards, when they were sitting at table, the lad sent to his lord, to desire he would let him have a cup of wine, for he was thirsty. The earl, rejoicing that he could drink, sent him a cup, blessed by the bishop, which, as soon as he had drunk, he immediately got up, shook off his infirmity, dressed himself, and going to the bishop, saluted him and the other guests, saying that he should be glad to eat and be merry with them. Being ordered, he sat down, ate, drank, and was merry, as if he had been one of the company; and living many years after, continued in the same state of health.'

Bishop John died, as has already been said, in 721 A.D., at the monastery he had founded in the great wood of Deira, called Inderwood, but now Beverley.

Legend has, however, many things to tell of marvels performed after his death, at his gorgeous shrine in the Minster, and elsewhere.

THE SHRINE OF ST. JOHN OF BEVERLEY AND THE PLEDGED SWORD.

In 937 A.D., two hundred and sixteen years after the death of St. John of Beverley, King Athelstane was on his way to chastise Constantine, King of Scotland, for countenance given to Godifed, a pagan Dane, who had attempted to seize Bernicia. Wulstan was, at that time, Abbot of Beverley, and a hastily summoned chapter of the brotherhood was held to see if, by some means, advantage could not be taken of the king's passage through the county to secure some benefits to the house. Godruff, the cellarer of the monastery, propounded a scheme, to which the consent of the chapter was ultimately given, for this purpose, and to its proposer was committed its execution. Shortly after, Godruff, with half a dozen companion monks, was on his way to meet the king in Lincolnshire. Surrounded by his chief men, Athelstane was approaching Lincoln at the head of his army. Riding thoughtfully along, he suddenly turned, and, addressing one of his officers, named Larwulf, said, 'Methinks, Larwulf, ours were a bootless errand unless we propitiate heaven in our favour.' 'Your sentiments, O king, are founded on wisdom and piety. Truly it behoves us to march under the protection of God's saints,' was the reply. 'Then,' said the king, 'this night we rest in Lincoln; to-morrow we will devote ourselves in the church there to fasting and prayer for guidance.' As they approached the city they suddenly, at a turn in the road, came upon a group of pilgrims loudly singing. They were dressed in blue woollen gowns, with leathern girdles, from which hung earthenware bottles; sandalled feet, heads bare, and with staves in their hands.

'Hold,' exclaimed the king, 'whom have we here?' and then, stopping and addressing the pilgrims, he said, 'Whence come ye? and what is the object of your anthem?' Their leader at once stepped forward, and replied, 'Know, O king, that once we were lame, blind, and afflicted in divers ways, and have been wandering about from one shrine to another without obtaining relief, until, by the favour of God, we chanced to come to that of St. John of Beverlega, where, after fasting and prayer, we were all, through the intercession of that glorified saint, restored to perfect health and strength, as thou now seest us, and we are returning to our homes chaunting the praise of our holy benefactor.' 'Wonderful!' exclaimed the king. 'And was it not, Larwulf, to the house of this holy man at Beverlega that we granted a charter in the first year of our reign?' 'It was,' replied the soldier. 'And it was as we were returning from chasing the Danes beyond the Roman wall that we were hospitably received at the monastery, and in return you granted the town of Beverlega sac and soc, and thol and theim, and exemption from the imposts of other towns.'

'I remember,' said Athelstane; 'and now my mind is changed. Instead of staying for fasting and prayer at Lincoln, I will haste on and seek the help of this St. John of Beverlega, for he appears a great and powerful saint. Do thou, Geoffrey of Sarum, lead the army forward to York and there await us; and thou, Larwulf, shalt accompany me to Beverlega. And you, ye reverend pilgrims, accept my thanks for your story, and take this gift, and erect therewith, in your own country, an oratory in honour of him who has been to you so great a benefactor.'

The army marched forward to York; the king and his lieutenant proceeded to the shrine at Beverley. The abbot had been warned of their approach and welcomed them to a grand banquet.

'Be seated, good father,' said the king, 'for I would confer with thee awhile.'

The abbot seated himself, and the king told him of the purpose of his visit to the north, of his encounter with the pilgrims, and then how, moved by their story, he had now turned aside to invoke the aid and blessing of St. John upon his enterprise. Wulstan applauded the king's wisdom. The king then stated that his time was short, for he must follow the army to York; he proposed, therefore, to visit the shrine, to prostrate himself and pray before it at midnight, and wished all the brotherhood, and the loyal men of Beverley, to join with him. At midnight a grand procession of monks, choristers, and others entered the holy house with banners and torches, Larwulf accompanying the king and carrying his sword reversed. Before the shrine he prostrated himself and prayed a long prayer, which

the chronicler gives, ending with the customary vow:
'That if success attended his arms, great, and still
more rich, gifts would he make to the church which
enshrined the relics of the saint, and, in pledge thereof,
he would now leave his sword upon the altar to be
redeemed by these princely donations upon his return.'
The banner of St. John was then delivered to Larwulf
to be carried before the king in battle. The procession
returned from the church, and early in the morning
Athelstane started to rejoin his army at York.

Soon after his departure Godruff and his companion
pilgrims returned to the abbey. Godruff, however, did
not long remain, but again departed on a journey to
the north.

It was on the eve of the battle of Brunnanburg.
Where that place is, or was, antiquarians have as yet
been unable to determine. The day had been hot,
and Athelstane and his army had marched far. They
had encamped by the side of a brook or river, and
there, in his tent, lay Athelstane, half awake—half
dreaming—anxious about the morrow. A slight noise
in the tent aroused him, and looking up,

'By the struggling moonbeam's misty light'

he saw dimly a venerable-looking figure, in a white
robe, and with long white hair hanging over his
shoulders, standing near his couch. His first impulse
was to seize his sword. 'Forbear, O king!' cried the
visitant; 'I come not to harm thee, but to grant thee
my blessing. Thy weapon is powerless against me;
reserve it for thy foes beyond the river.' Raising
himself up, the king said, 'Who art thou, and what

wantest thou?' 'List, O king,' was the reply, 'and be not afraid. I am he whose help thou sought at Beverlega. Thy prayer is ascended to heaven and thy petition is granted: lead thy army across the river to-morrow and victory shall be thine. Farewell! Ascribe to a higher power than thine own sword thy success, and forget not thy vow and thy pledge at my tomb.'

Athelstane looked again, but the figure was gone. He called the sentinel, and asked who had entered or left his tent, and was assured that no one had been near it. The king, therefore, was convinced that he had seen a vision, and that his visitor had been no one but St. John himself, and he was now fully at rest as to the result of the morrow. Nor was he disappointed. He gained a decisive victory, and the Scots and their king fled beyond the Tweed, whither Athelstane followed and compelled submission and homage. He then returned southward again, and called to redeem his sword, pledged on the altar at Beverlega. He was welcomed by the brotherhood, to whom Godruff had already brought tidings of success. The latter, however, avoided the royal presence, but one day by chance the king came upon him. 'Who art thou?' said the king. 'I thought I knew the features of all the brethren here by this time.' 'I am,' replied the cellarer, 'an humble brother, who has been living in seclusion by reason of a vow.' 'Yet thy features are familiar to me,' continued the king. 'Thou art marvellously like St. John, who appeared to me in vision on the eve of the battle.' Godruff was a little disconcerted, but soon was cool enough to reply: 'It may be so, my lord, for I am descended from the same family, and the likeness has been before remarked.' The king was satisfied; and before his departure he addressed the abbot and his brethren in redemption of his pledge in this princely fashion: 'In your church shall be founded a college of canons, endowed with ample possessions. It shall be a sanctuary, with a Fridstool before the altar, as a place of refuge and safety for debtors and criminals. Four stones, each a mile distant from this place, shall mark the bounds of the privileged ground. Your monastery shall be extended, and revenues increased, and the shrine of the Blessed John be amongst the most magnificent in the land.' To the town, also, he granted many and valuable privileges, and from that time it grew and flourished.

The monastery and church grew in magnificence and riches. Gifts poured in to the shrine of St. John, until it was embellished with gold and precious stones as few others have exceeded. Pilgrims in thousands, rich and poor, kings, nobles and peasants, resorted unto it. The banner of St. John, with those of St. Wilfrid of Ripon and St. Peter of York, formed the standard under which the Scots were so disastrously defeated near Northallerton in 1138 A.D. Even so late as the fifteenth century its fame, and the fame of the saint, had by no means diminished. At the battle of Agincourt (1415 A.D.), St. John was said to have appeared in the ranks of the English army, sitting on a white horse, and encouraged the men with many gracious words. At the same time the relics at Beverley were moved in sympathy, for on that day drops of blood exuded from the tomb. Henry V., on his return to England, accompanied by his queen, visited the church to worship at the shrine of the saint who had so aided in the battle. At length the time came when the Tudor eagle (or vulture?) swooped down upon the shrine of St. John, monastery and college, church and sanctuary, and left but the beautiful minster—denuded of all that could be borne away—without even the miserable pittance, left in other cases, for a parish priest to minister at its altar.

Legends connected with St. William of York.

Though separated in their lives by an interval of more than four hundred years, some of the legendary stories connected with St. John of Beverley and St. William of York are ascribed sometimes to the one and sometimes to the other, and some stories connected with St. William are, evidently, only amplified accounts of similar ones belonging to St. John. The legends of St. William seem, therefore, naturally to follow on to those of the older saint.

In 1140 A.D. died Archbishop Thurston of York. After some difficulty about the choice of his successor, the Chapter of York, in January of the following year, elected William Fitz-Herbert, who for ten years, at least, had been their treasurer. He was a man of noble family, his father being Count Herbert, treasurer to Henry I., and his mother a grand-daughter of the Conqueror and sister to King Stephen. An objection was raised to the validity of his election, chiefly by the abbots of the Cistercian monasteries in Yorkshire, and although the king (Stephen) invested him with the temporalities of the see, and he was duly consecrated by the English bishops, he failed to obtain more than a conditional sanction from the pope to his elevation.

After six or seven years of recrimination, the pope, by his usurped power over the English Church, removed him from the archbishopric, and ordered the Bishop of Durham and Chapter of York to elect another man to fill his place. They nominated two, of whom Murdac, Abbot of Fountains, was selected by the pope. Thus Murdac, with the approval of the pope (Eugenius), but without that of the king, stepped into the northern primacy. William, however, continued to enjoy the popular favour, and Murdac found his position anything but a bed of roses. William took refuge with his uncle, the Bishop of Winchester, residing at one of whose manors he received all the honours that could be paid to an archbishop. All classes regarded him, as an injured man, with affection and compassion. He lived as much as possible in retirement, spending his time in study and devotions. Not a murmur or harsh word against the pope, or others who had wronged him, escaped his lips. Thus passed the five years that Murdac held the archbishopric. In 1153 that prelate died.

The York Chapter again nominated William for his successor. William hastened to Rome, and this time with better success. The new pope (Anastatius), moved by the account of his trials, restored to him the position of which he had been deprived, and gave him 'the pall.' In the spring of 1154 he returned to take repossession of his see. He reached the city of York on the 9th of May, amid the rejoicing of an enormous and enthusiastic crowd. He was only spared to his people about a month, for on Trinity Sunday, while ministering at the service in the minster, he was taken ill, and, after lingering eight days, he died on June 8th. His death was ascribed, by some, to poison in the sacramental wine, but in all probability it was due to fever. His body was interred in the nave of the minster. His meekness, his sufferings, his wrongs, and, finally, his tragic end, only exalted his memory in the popular mind.

Many miracles soon were ascribed to him in life, and to his mediation after death. From his tomb flowed the holy oil, as from that of John of Beverley, and other saints.

As yet York had no saint exclusively its own. John of Beverley had been its bishop, but his shrine was at Beverley. In 1227 A.D. a movement was made to obtain the canonization of William. It was, however, about fifty years later before this was done by Pope Nicholas III. Perhaps the most magnificent gathering of royalty, nobles, and ecclesiastics that ever York minster has witnessed took place on the 8th of January, 1283 A.D., at the translation of the bones of the saint from their resting-place in the nave to the shrine prepared for them behind the high altar. Edward I. and his queen were present, surrounded by their court.

From this time, until swept away at the Reformation, the shrine of St. William occupied a prominent place in the devotions of the people of the north, though never so high a one, perhaps, as that of St.

John of Beverley. Legends tell of thirty-six marvels wrought through him. They are recorded in the magnificent window known as St. William's window, in the north aisle of the minster. Only a few of them need be repeated here; but the following general remarks by the Rev. J. T. Fowler in his description ('Yorkshire Archæological Journal,' vol. iii.) of this window will be read with interest:

'Among the fifty compartments (of the window) representing miracles of St. William are several representing miracles of St. John of Beverley.' . . . The most probable explanation of this co-mingling seems to be as follows: ' Until the acquisition of St. William as patron saint of York, St. John of Beverley, Archbishop of York in the eighth century, held that position. The right of sanctuary enjoyed by Beverley at that period, and which gave it another ground of precedence, was connected with the repose there of the relics of St. John. On any great emergency the York clergy were in the habit of going to Beverley, to appeal in person to the clemency of their patron.' This is clear, not to mention other instances, from an account in the 'Acta Sanctorum,' written before the time of St. William, of the clergy of York, on one occasion, when there was a great drought, having gone to Beverley to implore the assistance of St. John. His feretory was carried in procession; the sky, before cloudless and serene, gradually became wild and overcast; rain fell in torrents to refresh the parched earth; and the monks went back to York full of praises towards, and confidence in, their glorious confessor. Nothing seems more natural, therefore, than that after the death of St. William and the beginning of miracles at his tomb, some at least of those of the earlier saint, with which the people were more familiar, should have gradually got mixed up with those of the latter, and, in days when books were few and instruction chiefly oral, should have become attributed to him.

'It was unreasonable that the saint of the metropolitan city should be outdone in miracles by the saint of Beverley, to say nothing of the natural tendency of later miracles to outshine those that go before. If St. John of Beverley cured a man of blindness, well, St. William gave back eyes to a man whose eyes had been bodily extracted and carried off, none knew where, by a boy of the name of Hugh. The same kind of thing happened elsewhere continually. Thus, at Bridlington, the miracles related of their St. John were as obviously taken and exaggerated from those of St. William, as some of the latter were from those of St. John of Beverley. Did a stone fall on the head of a man in the presence of St. William, with far greater audacity it fell upon that of St. John of Bridlington himself. Did a man fall from a step-ladder, but recover on the approach of St. William, he fell from the top of a house, was smashed to pieces, killed, but brought back to life by the intercession of St. John. Did St. William once recover a child that had fallen into the Ouse, and was supposed by the bystanders to be dead, St. John brought back to life several who had been really dead for many hours. Did St. William heal one who had swallowed a harmless frog, St. John restored one who had swallowed a venomous spider; and so on. These examples, which might be greatly multiplied, will tend to show how earnestly the custodians of the later shrines laboured to acquire a glory for them surpassing, if it might be, that of the earlier.'

THE BROKEN BRIDGE.

When William, lately restored to his archbishopric, arrived at York on the 8th of May, 1154 A.D., an immense and enthusiastic multitude met him. As they were passing over Ouse Bridge—a wooden structure in those days—the weight and turbulence of the crowd caused the fastenings at the end to be broken. The whole structure gave way, and an innumerable multitude of 'men, women, and children,' mingled with harnessed horses, fell in confusion into the rapid stream where it was deepest. A great cry of agony arose from the drowning host. 'The archbishop, turning towards those who were immersed in the water, made the sign of the cross over the people everywhere overwhelmed by the waves, and, dissolved in tears, offered prayers to God asking deliverance, that the tempest of the waves might not drown them, nor the deep swallow them up, nor the gladness of these men praising God be turned into deadly hurt.' No sooner was the prayer uttered, than the surging waters became themselves as a bridge, on which all who had fallen in were conveyed to the solid ground. As an old York breviary says:

> 'Unda ruens populum recipit ruentem,
> Et se pontem efficit per omnipotentem.'

Not one person was lost. One chronicle even says, in order to be very minute: 'Not one was hurt, except that the leg of a certain horse was broken.' In memory, it is said, of this miracle was erected the chapel dedicated to St. William on Ouse Bridge, York, which was only taken down, on the rebuilding of the bridge, in very modern times.

The miracle of the broken bridge has been, by a few ancient writers, claimed for Ferrybridge, or some other spot in the neighbourhood of Pontefract, and thus accounting for the somewhat peculiar name of that town. Whatever may have been the origin of that name, modern research has shown that the miracle by St. William at the broken bridge cannot be appropriated to explain it, since charters and other documents have been found denominating the place 'Pons fractus' many years before the date of the miracle at York.

EYES GIVEN TO THE BLIND.

To the brief or petition to the pope in 1226, for the canonization of William of York, we are indebted for the following legend. A man named Ralph, being accused of having broken the king's peace, was subjected to trial by wager of battle. His adversary was named Besing. Ralph was overcome, and in the duel one of his eyes was put out. As a punishment for his transgression—now proved by being vanquished in wager of battle—he was condemned to be deprived of the other eye. The executioner carried out this sentence, and a lad named Hugh picked up both eyes and carried them away. Ralph, being thus unjustly, as he knew, punished, spent some days in fasting and prayer, and then came to the tomb of the Blessed William, and received back two eyes, smaller, and of a different colour than his former ones, but giving him again sharp and clear sight.

THE ORDEAL OF FIRE.

The following is a somewhat similar story to the last one. Two women were charged with having caused the death of a third person. While in prison awaiting trial one of the accused died. The other, on the coming of the king's justices, was brought forth and charged with the crime. She denied that she had anything to do with it; but she was adjudged to make proof of innocence or guilt by the ordeal, which was then, according to the custom of the kingdom, that of taking in her hand a piece of red-hot iron.

This ordeal has been thus described: The iron, when sufficiently hot, was placed upon a pillar at one end of a space of nine feet. The accused immediately grasped the iron in his hand, took three strides to the other end of the space, threw down the iron, and fled to an altar appointed, where a priest bound up his hand in clean white linen cloths, sealed it with the seal of the church, kept it so sealed for three days, and at the end of that time opened the cloths. If the man's hand was then found whole he thanked God; but if, on the contrary, a sore was found on the track of the iron, he was accounted guilty.

In the instance of the woman in the legend, after she had thus borne the iron, a blister, of about the size of half a walnut, was found in her hand. Wherefore, being so burnt by the fire, she was declared guilty and sentenced to death for the homicide, and delivered over to the officers for execution. But, before the sentence was carried out, she obtained permission to pray, and for this purpose to visit the tomb of the Blessed William. Immediately she entered the sacred space around the tomb, the blister vanished so completely that no trace of it could be found. This was reported to the principal justices of the kingdom. They at once judged the woman absolved and innocent, and set her at liberty, saying that since God and the saints had absolved her, neither would they condemn her. They, however, handed over the justices who had condemned her to the mercy of the king, 'because they had used false-witness, and given unjust judgment against her who bore the red-hot iron in the cathedral church of York before the altar of the Blessed Michael, whom, and whose hand, the twelve officers, the executioners, examined and wished to drag from the church as guilty; but the priest, the keeper of the tomb, wished to prevent being taken forth, having been cured by a miracle of the Blessed William.'

SIGHT GIVEN TO A BLIND GIRL.

A young girl of the parish of Leeds, having lost her sight in early childhood, was for seven years in total darkness. Led by the hand of a hired guide, she came to the tomb of St. William, in order that she might be cured. She remained there a long time in prayer and weeping. During the holy night of Pentecost she lay down to sleep, and, whilst neither quite awake or fast asleep, there appeared to her one most beautiful to look upon, having the white hair of an angel, in comparison with whose raiment snow was black, fragrant with unspeakable perfumes, who, having pity on her misery, touched the pupils of her eyes, and, at the touch of his hand, the darkness of blindness cleared away, and for gloomy night was given her cheerful day. This is said to have taken place on Whitsunday, June 12th, 1177 A.D., and that Paulinus, priest of Leeds, and the parishioners, and the mother of the girl were witnesses to its truth.

Many other such legends are extant and might be given, such as that of the healing of a paralytic clerk from Weskburgh; of a dropsical man from Harewood; a dumb girl, daughter of a glazier, from Rokesburgh; of a woman poisoned by eating a frog, etc.

The following is of somewhat a different character. It is represented in a portion of St. William's window, and ascribed to either that saint or St. John of Beverley.

THE YOUNG STUDENT.

A young scholar once went to Beverley to study divinity, and charmed the monks there, not less by his attainments and manners than by his real worth and industry. The devil, envying his good name and reputation, set a trap whereby to ensnare him. In an unhappy hour his eyes rested on the face of a beautiful virgin of the city, and his heart steadfastly inclined to her. Day by day his love for her increased and that for his books diminished, until at last he became like a horse or mule, in which is no understanding, and his beautiful face was spoiled by leanness. Despairing of all other modes of release or cure, he took himself to the Blessed John, who effectually released him from the snare of the evil one and restored him to his accustomed health.

These legendary miracles in the middle ages are, perhaps, best regarded as somewhat on a par with the reputed marvels of spiritualism, animal magnetism, etc., of our own—supposed to be—less superstitious times. The minds of all classes in those days were prepared to believe such marvels from such sources; and when imagination, or hysteria, and possibly, in some instances, fraud supplied the incidents, the popular mind believed and propagated them. Is it quite certain that the popular mind of this nineteenth century has much room to cast a stone at that of those —in some things certainly—darker ages?

The Horn of Ulphus.

Among the treasures and curiosities preserved at York minster is the celebrated horn of Ulphus. This most interesting relic of the old Saxon, or Danish times, is really not a horn at all, but a portion of the tusk of an elephant, about three feet long. Round the thick end are engraved, with beautiful workmanship, a number of emblematic figures, in some respects not unlike those found on Egyptian and Assyrian monuments. The horn was richly mounted with gold, until it fell into the hands of some of the desecrators of things ancient and holy at the time of the Commonwealth, who took it away and appropriated the gold upon it. Towards the end of the seventeenth century it was in the hands of Lord Fairfax (Henry), nephew of the General, and by him was restored, in 1675 A.D., to the minster authorities. They, at the same time, caused it to be reset with the brass silver-gilt setting which it now bears, in place of the gold with which it had been previously adorned.

The legend, or tradition, connected with the horn is, that a certain Ulphus, son of Thoraldi, was king, or sub-king, of the western portion of Deira, in the days when the Danes ruled their Saxon brethren in these parts. Of Ulphus's four sons, Adelbert, the eldest, was slain in battle, and the others, even in their father's lifetime, quarrelled and strove about the succession to his estates and kingdom. Wearied by their strife, the aged chieftain at last determined on a step that would end their disputes, treat them all alike, and be to the benefit of his dependents, and that was, to give the whole of his dominions to the Church. He therefore rode to York, taking with him his largest drinking-horn, and, filling it with wine, he went upon his knees before the high altar, there drank off the contents, and then placed the horn upon the altar, to be held by the Church as title, in all time, to all his lands, tenements, and wealth, thus bestowed upon God and St. Peter. These lands included four carucates of land in the historical parish of God-mundham, which now, or lately did, belong to the Minster.

The legend has been more fully told, and told well, in the following poetical version of it by Reid Tranmar in ' Legends of York, and other Poems :'

' O'er the wealthy West Deira, in the stormy days of old,
Ulphus reigned, the son of Thorald, wise and merciful and bold ;
But the king was not immortal, tho' of patriarchal mould.

'With the failing weight of Nature bowed his many-wintered head,
And his sons began to argue who should reign when he were dead,
While the people wept and murmured; "We shall be oppressed," they said.

' Now there was a royal maiden, daughter of an elder son,
Adelbert, who died in battle, leaving her—a precious one—
Orphan to his father Ulphus, ere her life was well begun.

' Ulphus troubled very sorely, called on Lady Adelwynne,
Led her to the palace garden, for they often walked therein;
Praised her lithely-rounded figure, and the whiteness of her skin:

' Twisted one by one her ringlets, calling her " My little joy!
Blue-eyed, like my wife Helena; how I wish thou wert a boy!"
" Dear my father," said the maiden, "I had wrought you some annoy:

' Either I had been too timid, for the people of the west,
Loved too much the power of riches, or the idleness of rest;
Or I might have been a tyrant; dear my father, it is best."

' Round the garden paced the monarch, leaning on the maiden's arm,
Leaning on her power of loving, charm of every other charm;
All abrupt; she stayed and reddened, smitten by a quick alarm.

' In the woven bower of willow Adelwynne so loved to keep,
Lay, at length, her uncle Kerdic, nerveless in a heavy sleep;
Near to him a fallen goblet told how he had drunken deep.

' Thro' the woven shade of willow came a line of sunny light,
Touched him with a fiery finger, pointing out the bitter sight—
Oh! how shame is yet more shameful in the day than in the night!

'Then King Ulphus, son of Thorald, cried—" Is *it* a son of mine?
Uprise, thou nidering sluggard! *Thou* to head a Royal line!
Never! never! Let us leave him! Adelwynne, the crown is thine!"

'But she said, "Not so, my father. Think, my lord, and turn again.
Were it well that I, a maiden, over Deira-land should reign,
When to wear the crown of Thorald both my uncles yet remain?

'"Torfrid comes to-day from hunting; Edmund from the north is bound;
They will meet and ride together. Hark! I hear a bugle sound!
Good my lord, again be merry. Lo! an heir is quickly found."

'Now with mingled men and banners came the companies in view;
In the van the royal leaders rode together clad in blue;
By the massy collars all the sons of Ulphus knew.

'Yet, altho' they rode together, not in love the brothers came;
Torfrid spoke, in words of thunder, things of bitterness and blame;
Edmund answered low and quiet, but his eye was all aflame.

'"Coward! liar! double-dealer! thus to win my love from me!"
Answered Edmund, "O word-smiter, was the world ordained for thee?
Is a lady, fair and wealthy, not to please her fancy free?"

'" She was mine by true betrothal ere I left the northern land."
"Ha!" said Edmund, inly laughing; "watchmen by the treasure stand;
Now I open hall and coffer with the key of her white hand."

'"Mine the gold and mine the tower; mine the lovely Gundelheid."
"Take the gold and take the tower; only give me back my bride!"
"Nay, my dear and loving brother, yet a little further ride."

'"Ride a hunting, mighty Torfrid; let another win the prize.
Gold is sweet, and so are kisses: both are given to the wise."
Answered Torfrid, "I am elder; wait until the father dies."

'"Oh! but I will waste thy borders; every stone shall lie in blood.
She shall kneel and sue before me, throwing back her silken hood;
And I will not spare, but slay thee, for revenge is very good."

'This King Ulphus, son of Thorald, heard, and looked upon the maid,
Where she listened very sadly close beside him in the shade.
"Yea," he said, "I *was* a father—Adelbert is lowly laid."

'Then she soothed him calm and gently, till he said, "Ah, maiden fair!
This thy gift of sympathizing, how it is a virtue rare.
Surely thou shalt guide the people; Adelwynne shall be mine heir.

'"Kerdic hath no wit but wine-wit; Torfrid is a son of Cain;
Edmund is a wily coward, and the dead come not again.
Thou shalt wed thy cousin Edwy, and, by Woden, thou shalt reign!"

'Blushed the girl from heart to forehead; "Swear not so, my lord," she said;
"What have we to do with Woden? Surely, since the dead be dead,
And the living be unworthy, yet there is an heir instead.

' "Give to Christ the land of Deira; let the Church the people
    guard;
So they all shall dwell securely, and thy spirit have reward;
Be not angered; think upon it, O my father and my lord!"

' "Yea, I will, mine own Rune-maiden; as thou sayest, it
    shall be;
Adelwynne, my little daughter, better than a son to me;
In thy face shines out the image of the Lord's prayer visibly."

' So King Ulphus, son of Thorald, knelt before the holy shrine
In the stately York Cathedral, and he quaffed a horn of wine,
Giving unto Christ the kingdom, saying, "This shall be the
    sign—

' "Keep my horn, O holy father; so, from age to age be
    known,
Power is a trust from heaven; kings have nothing of their
    own;
Never shall a son unworthy sit upon my father's throne."

'Stranger, when you mark the token, once beset with heavy
    gold,
Stripped by avaricious fingers, re-adorned as you behold—
Think upon the gift of Ulphus in the stormy days of old.'

A Legend of St. Cuthbert and Ripon Monastery.

Eata, Abbot of Melrose, was given, about the year 660 A.D., by Alchfrid, King of Deira, lands at Ripon whereon to build and maintain a monastic establishment. Taking with him some of the brethren from Melrose, what is known as 'The Old Abbey of Ripon' soon sprung up under their hands. Among the brethren who accompanied Eata from Melrose was one named Cuthbert, and in the new foundation

Cuthbert was appointed to the office of guest-master. The legend of his entertaining, in that capacity, an angel of the Lord cannot be more graphically told than in the language of Bede, the historian, who has preserved it:

'On going out early in the morning from the inner buildings of the monastery to the guest-chamber, he found a young man sitting there, and supposing he was mortal, he immediately welcomed him with the customary forms of kindness. He gave him water to wash his hands, he himself bathed his feet, he wiped them with a napkin, and he placed them in his bosom, humbly chafing them with his hands; and he asked him to remain until the third hour of the day, that he might then be refreshed with food, lest if he should go on his journey without support, he should suffer alike from hunger and winter's cold. For he thought that the stranger had been wearied with a night journey, as well as by the snowy blasts, and that he had turned aside there at dawn for the sake of resting. The other answered that he could not do so, and said that he must speedily depart, for the abode to which he was hastening was very far distant. But Cudberet persevered in his entreaties, and at last, adjuring him in the Divine name, he obliged him to stay; and immediately after the prayers of the hour of tierce were concluded and meal-time was at hand, he laid the table and offered him food, saying, "I beseech thee, brother, refresh thyself until I return from having brought some new bread, for I expect it is ready baked by this time." But when he returned he found not the guest whom he had left at table, and, looking out for the print of his feet, he saw none whatever, although a recent fall of snow had covered the ground, and would very readily have betrayed the steps of the traveller and pointed out the direction which he had taken. The man of God, therefore, greatly amazed, and wondering inwardly at the circumstance, replaced the table in the inner apartment. On entering this he forthwith perceived the fragrance of a marvellous sweet savour, and on looking round to see whence so sweet an odour arose, he saw lying beside him three loaves, yet warm, of unwonted whiteness and beauty. And trembling, he said within himself, "I perceive that this is an angel of God whom I have received, who has come to feed, and not to be fed. Lo! he has brought such loaves as this earth cannot produce, for they surpass lilies in whiteness, roses in smell, and honey in flavour. Hence it is clear that they have not sprung from this heavy earth of ours, but have been brought from the paradise of Eden. And no marvel that he who enjoys the eternal bread of life in heaven should refuse to partake of earthly food." Wherefore the man of God, being moved to compunction from having been witness to so mighty a miracle, was more zealous from that time forth in the works of virtue, till, with increasing good deeds, heavenly grace also increased. And from that time he very often was allowed to see and converse with angels, and when an hungred he was refreshed with food specially prepared for him by the Lord.'

Legends of St. Robert, the Hermit of Knaresborough.

Robert, the hermit of Knaresborough, was a native of York, born about 1160 A.D., and, after trying a monk's life at Newminster Abbey, in Northumberland, he settled down to a hermit's life near Knaresborough.

For many years he lived there, inhabiting, for the greater part of the time, a cave about one mile to the south-east of the town, still known as St. Robert's Cave; though on two or three occasions, for short periods, he took up his abode at other spots in the vicinity.

At first he had for a companion a certain St. Giles—who, indeed, he found inhabiting the cave at his coming.

There are three accounts of his life extant: one in Latin triplets, and probably the work of a monk of Fountains; another metrical one, in old English; and a third in Latin prose. These are all put under contribution for the following legends, most of which have already appeared in 'Lays and Leaves of the Forest,' where a full history of the hermit is given.

St. Giles, his companion in the hermitage, soon grew tired either of the life or of his companion, and returned to his family; and so the old metrical life relates that

> 'Longer liked him not that life,
> But as a wretch went to his wife;
> As hound that casts off his kit,
> And, aye, turns and taketh his vomit.'

Robert also, apparently tired of his dwelling, besought

from a wealthy lady of the neighbourhood a small chapel and hermitage known as St. Hilda's, a short distance from Knaresborough. Thither he removed, but resided there only about a year; for, being attacked by thieves, he thought it best to abandon everything to them:

> 'It befell upon a night,
> Fell thieves came with main and might;
> His bower they brak, and bare away
> His bread, his cheese, his sustenance,
> And his poore men's purveyance.
> Havand in his mind always,
> How God his gospel says,
> "If fools pursue you, false and fell,
> In a city where you dwell,
> Flee unto another than."
> Therefore Robert raise and ran,
> And sped him unto Spofford town,
> To sue God with devocione.'

After a time, however, and after trying to live with the monks at Hedley, in the parish of Bramham, but

> 'On him they raise all in a route,
> And bade this blessed man go out,'

he returned to St. Hilda's.

There he was one day sleeping in the flowery grass, when his mother, who had lately died, appeared to him:

> 'A time as St. Robert lay
> In a meadow—time of May,
> In flowers, slep and in a stede,
> Appeared his mother, that was dead,
>   Pale and wan of hide and hue.'

She told him that, for usury and other sins, she was suffering great torments, and must continue to do so until set free through his prayers. This greatly troubled him, and for a whole year he ceased not to make intercession on her behalf. At the end of that time she again appeared to him, with a happy and smiling face, to thank him and announce her deliverance:

> ' And blissed her bain that made her blithe,
> Go! and, my son, now shall I swithe;
> Wend to wealth that never shall wane;
> Farewell! I bless thee, blood and bain!'

The hermit was again disturbed at St. Hilda, for William de Stuteville,

> ' Lord of that land, both east and west,
> Of frith, and field, and of forest,'

was riding through his domains, and came upon Robert's ' honeste halle.' He asked of his attendants, ' Whose was that building?' They replied ' that it belonged to

> ' Ane hermite, that is perfite,
> Robert, that is no rebellour,
> A servante of oure Savioure.'

'No,' replied the baron, ' not so, but an abettor and harbourer of thieves.' Then he ordered the place to be demolished, and the hermit banished from the forest. The attendants were most unwilling to molest ' the holy hermite,' and delayed to execute the order. But Stuteville passed the same way a few days afterwards, and, seeing the buildings yet standing, was mad with fury, and ordered their instant destruction:

> 'Then they durst no langer byde,
> But unto Robert's housying hyed,
> And dang them down, baith less and maire,
> Nothing left they standing there.'

Again by violence deprived of his dwelling, Robert for some time wandered from place to place in the forest, but at length returned to the shelter of the cliffs near Knaresborough—probably not, however, to his original cave, but to an excavation in the rock, which is now known as St. Robert's Chapel, and also as the Chapel of St. Giles.

Here he formed himself a dwelling, at the front of the cave, by means of stakes and boughs of trees. And hither

> 'High and low unto him hyed,
> In soth for to be edifyed.'

But again his enemy, the lord of the adjoining castle, passed that way

> 'Withe hound, and hawke upon his hand;'

and, seeing the smoke curling up from Robert's hut, he again asked, 'Who dwelt there?' The reply was, 'Robert the Hermit.' 'What! that same Robert whom I not long ago expelled from my forest?' Again he was answered, 'It is the same.' Then he sware a mad oath that he should at once be driven away again:

> 'Saying he would his house destroy;
> Wait in a cave, and him annoy;
> Wolves he'd bring, and them employ
>   Out from his hiding-place.

> ' Then our Robert, on this hearing,
> "Well, you know," says he, nought fearing,
> "Hence no wolf, God-right revering,
>   Shall ever me displace." '

But the Lord of Knaresborough soon was made to repent of his temerity in again seeking to disturb the hermit. In the middle of the following night there appeared to him a terrible vision. Three men, 'blacker than Ynd,' stood by him in his chamber. Two of them carried a fearful instrument of torture, and the third—a tall, powerful man—had in his hand two iron clubs. This man bade the baron rise and take one of the clubs and defend himself, 'for the wrongs with which thou spitest the man of God, because I am sent here to fight thee on his part.'

> ' Fears the lord—his whole frame shakes,
> Horror deep his mind o'ertakes,
> Vanished they as he awakes,
>   Who rushed in wrath to rend him.'

The hermit's dwelling was saved. As soon as the morning dawned, Stuteville hastened to the cell, and

> ' In the cavern he low bow'd,
> His transgression disallowed.
> Gave the land, an owner proud,
>   To Robert and his guest-friends.'

His enemy's ire was thus turned to the saint's advantage, and henceforth he dwelt at peace with him.

Again the hermit removed—this time from his hut in front of St. Robert's Chapel to his original cave, some little distance further down the river. He was about this time visited by his brother Walter, who had risen to be Mayor of York, and who caused to be built for him a small chapel in front of the cave, known as the Chapel of the Holy Cross, the foundations of which are yet to be seen.

St. Robert here again took to himself a companion—one named Ivo, said to have been a Jew. But neither did Ivo and Robert long dwell together in amity, but, yielding to the temptation of Satan, we are told

> 'Ivo with Robert soon had strife,
> So withdraws from desert life.'

But as he was making haste in his escape, in passing through a wood he stepped on a rotten bough, which caused him to fall into a ditch and break his leg. Robert, being aware of the accident, hastened to the spot, and, smiling at Ivo's plight, rebuked him for his fault, and reminded him that 'no one putting his hand to the plough, and looking back, is fit for the kingdom of God.' Ivo humbly confessed his error in deserting his friend, and begged his pardon. Robert bid him—

> 'Wretched, seek my habitation,
> Blessed and free for contemplation,
> Long and long God's domination,
>   Thou by thy prayer hast won.'

He then touched the backslider's leg, and it was restored sound and strong. They never parted more until Robert died, and were worthy brothers in self-mortification.

The wild animals of the forest were completely at the hermit's beck and call. Once, when collecting alms, he asked the lord of the forest for a cow. One, so wild and ferocious that no one dare approach her, was given him. At once he went after her into the forest, and, going up to her, put a band round her neck, and led her home gentle as a lamb. One of the attendants, seeing the animal so easily tamed, proposed to get her back from the hermit by subtlety. The master did not approve of the attempt; nevertheless the man determined to make it. He went to Robert as a beggar, with distorted face and counterfeited lameness in both hands and feet, and telling a piteous tale of wife and children dying for want, implored him to give him the cow. 'God gave, and God shall have,' was the reply; 'but it shall be with thee as thou hast feigned.' So when the counterfeit cripple would have driven off his prize, he found himself so lame both in hands and feet that he was unable to move. Seeing this judgment upon him, the man cried out, 'O Robert, thou servant of God, forgive my trespass and the injury I have done!' He was instantly forgiven, and the use of his limbs restored to him. This story, and the following one, formed the subjects of coloured windows set up in Knaresborough Church in 1473 A.D., 250 years after the hermit's death.

Robert suffered great damage by the stags from Knaresborough Forest breaking down and trampling his corn and other crops:

> 'Often stags made fierce attacks,
> Cut up cornfields in their tracks;
> All the earth their wildness racks,
> Except where each one rests.'

Again Robert went to the lord of the forest, and desired that they might be restrained. 'I give thee full permission,' replied De Stuteville, 'to shut them up in thy barn.'

> ' Answers he with ill design,
> " Christian, shut up the stags as thine,
> That with chaunts thou mayest refine
> Them yet untam'd by pains." '

Robert, taking a small stick in his hand, proceeded into the fields, and drove the wild deer into his barn like so many lambs, and shut them up.

> ' Seeks he the plain, his barn is filled,
> Stags being brought from fields well tilled,
> Joining in, as beasts well skilled,
> They snort with hallowed chime.'

He then went to inform the baron what he had accomplished, and desired to know what next should be done with them.

Finding that more had been done than was intended, permission was only given him to retain three of them for use of oxen to draw his plough. Robert thanked the donor, and went home and yoked them to his plough. Their submission and docility at this work were daily seen and admired by all who passed by.

More than once he had to contend with Satanic visitants in his cell. One:

> ' About his house this harlotte hyed,
> His devocions he defied;
> All the vessels that he fand
> He tyfled and touched them with his hand—
> His pott, his panne, his sauce, his fowle,
> With his fingers fat and foule.'

The details of these visitations are perhaps better untold. Suffice it to say, that the visitant was once driven away by being sprinkled with holy water, once by the sign of the cross, and finally by the hermit's 'most hallowed staff.'

In 1203 A.D. De Stuteville, lord of the castle and forest of Knaresborough, died, and for his good deeds was buried at Fountains Abbey. The charge of these royal possessions was soon after handed over by King John to Sir Brian de Lisle, who, proving a great friend to Robert, induced the king (John) with his Court, when he came to hunt in the royal forest, to visit him in his cell. The king came with a great concourse of nobles. When they entered, the hermit was at prayer, prostrate before the altar of his chapel. He did not rise, though aware of the presence and dignity of his visitors, until De Lisle went to him and whispered, 'Brother Robert, arise quickly; our lord King John is here, desirous to see thee.' Then he arose and said, 'Show me which of these is my king.' One of his peers, 'a knight, outpoured much talk, and this beside:

'" Ask the king out of his store
Thee to bless this day with more;
That by his grant here, as before,
You may with yours abide."'

He declined to do so; but, taking up an ear of corn from the floor, he addressed the king: 'Art thou able, O my king, by thy power, to create such an ear as this out of nothing?' The king replied he was unable to do so. 'Then there is no king,' answered Robert, 'but the Lord only.' Some of the attendants said, 'This man is mad;' others, 'Nay; he is wiser than we, since he is the servant of God, in whom is all wisdom.' John was not offended, but rather pleased at the blunt address of St. Robert, and said to him, 'Ask of me whatever is necessary for thee, and it shall be given.'

> 'Answered Robert thus the speaker—
> "Silver and gold to me, Christ's seeker,
> Earthly gifts none can be weaker
> To meet our transient need."'

But Ivo, when the king had departed, finding that no alms had been taken, and mindful also of their successors, ran or sent after him, and the king conferred upon them as much land of the waste in the adjacent woods, as they could cultivate with one plough, by way of alms to the poor, and also free liberty to cut and take firewood and bedding.

St. Robert died September 24th, 1218 A.D., and after a quarrel between Ivo, his companion, and the monks of Fountains about the disposal of his body, it was buried by Ivo. As he and other brethren committed it to the tomb, multitudes gathered, from all the country round, to pay the last honours to one who had been to them so great a benefactor:

> 'Crowds are round with cowl and hood,
> Poor, and powerful, and good,
> Him to mourn in sorrowing mood,
> Maids, husbands, widows, seek.

> 'Who from wolves our loved homes freed?
> Who for his own did intercede?
> Who with words our souls did feed?
> Thus grieved, they ever speak.

> 'Ivo next, with greatest care,
> Did, with much beside, prepare
> (Himself and many a helper there),
> In earth our saint to place.'

The saint was thus buried where he had desired, in the Chapel of the Holy Cross, built for him by his brother, 'in a tomb before the altar.'

Many of these legends have been depicted in the glass of the churches at Knaresborough and elsewhere. A window of six lights, all filled with scenes from the life of St. Robert, is still to be seen in Morley Church, near Derby. From his tomb is said to have issued (as from that of St. John of Beverley, and others) the holy oil; and the shrine was for long—though not, perhaps, to the extent of some of those of the more notorious mediæval saints—a place of pilgrimage for the feeble and lame, the deaf and blind, in their superstition or search of healing.

III.

LEGENDS OF SATANIC AGENCY.

LEGENDS, attributing marvels in the physical world to the agency of the powers of evil, are numerous in all lands. Whatever seemed beyond human power to accomplish, or was inexplicable as to its origin or purpose, was, in the middle ages, almost certain to be set down as a work of the devil, and as such, in popular tradition, has been handed down to our own times. And these stories, frequently, still hold their own against all that the teaching of science, or the progress of discovery, can say to the contrary.

Legends of this class are numerous in Yorkshire and elsewhere; many of them have many characteristics in common, and often it is evident that one, relating to a particular place or object, has been appropriated and applied to other places and objects of like character, and thus the story has been multiplied many times over.

A few only of this class of legend will be here related.

THE DEVIL'S ARROWS OR BOLTS.

Near to Aldborough, the ancient *Iseur* of the British, and *Isurium* of the Roman times, and still nearer to the more modern town of Boroughbridge, stand three stone obelisks (formerly there were four), which have in all historic times taxed the curiosity of observers, and the ingenuity of inquirers, to account for the manner in which they have come to be where they are, and for their original object or purpose.

They are massive stone pillars—calculated to weigh from 30 to 36 tons each—standing upright in a line running nearly north and south, the second at the distance of 66 yards from the first, and the third at 120 yards from the second, each having about two yards of its base embedded in the earth. They are known as the Devil's Bolts, or the Devil's Arrows, and legend thus explains their name, and—what learned men have yet been unable satisfactorily to do—their origin and original use also.

In the days when *Iseur* was the capital of the Brigantine Kingdom, and the king of that powerful British tribe reigned in that city, there came thither a small band of the first Christian missionaries who visited this country.

They expounded before the king and his nobles their new doctrine, and exhorted them to forsake their Druidical gods and become followers of Christ. The king appointed a conference, at which he would preside, of his chiefs, the Druids of his kingdom, and the missionaries. This was held near Roulstone Scar, on the slope of the Hambleton Hills.

As the discussion was proceeding, and the cause of the Christian teachers was winning its way, the assembly was joined by a strange Druid of commanding and venerable appearance. At the king's request this stranger took a place among them, and listened to the further exposition of the new faith. He then arose, and by gibe and taunt and sneer ridiculed the teaching of the strangers, and upheld the tenets and advantages of Druidism so effectually that a murmur of applause ran through the assembly. When he sat down the king arose and said: 'Venerable priest, thou speakest well; thy words are truth. These strangers must now leave our shores and return to the land whence they came, for we are unable to accept what they conceive to be truth.'

Fortunately, however, one of the missionaries had noticed, as this venerable arch-Druid had raised his garment somewhat by the earnestness of his action while speaking, that his feet appeared to be sinking into the rock on which he stood, and that the hard stone was partly liquified around them. At once it flashed upon the observer's mind who the opponent was with whom they had to deal. He there and then challenged him as the great arch-fiend—the enemy of all righteousness—against whom they had been warning the assembly, and cried in a stern voice: 'Satan, I defy thee! In the name of Him whom thou hast reviled, I command thee to show thyself who thou art, and to depart to the hell whence thou camest!'

At once he was unmasked, and stood forth in all his hideousness in the sight of all present. Then amid sulphurous emanations, and the execrations of those who had so nearly been his dupes, he took his flight. But, being unable to extricate his feet from the semi-molten rock on which he stood, he bore away with him a large mass of that rock adhering to them, until, in passing over How Hill, some six or seven miles to the west of *Iseur*, the mass became loosened and dropped to the ground.

Some time afterwards he conceived the idea of turning to account his late burden, as an instrument for the annihilation of the now Christian city of *Iseur*. He therefore re-winged his flight to How Hill, cut up the mass of rock into four large ' bolts ' or ' arrows,' and, planting his feet firmly, one on the front and the other behind the hill, he addressed the doomed town in the words, which some more mundane being must have heard, for they have ever since been reported from mouth to mouth;

> ' Borobrigg, Borobrigg,
>   Keep out of the way,
>   For Auldboro' town
>   I'll ding down to-day.'

And then he hurled—we are not told whether with his hands, after the manner of hurling a javelin, or as bolts from a gigantic crossbow, or as arrows from a long bow—but somehow, he hurled the ponderous stones at the town. They were all, however, by some means, intercepted when far short of their goal, and fell, each in the place it has since occupied, one end firmly embedding itself in the earth and keeping the rest in an upright, or nearly upright, position, memorials for all time of the impotence of Satan's wrath, and of his intended evil averted from the faithful city.

The similarity of this story to one in Ireland is very remarkable. Close to the ancient city of Cashel, in Tipperary, is an enormous isolated mass of rock known as the Rock of Cashel. Upon it stands some of the most interesting ruins in that historically interesting country. At the foot of this rock is a detached portion, smaller, but weighing many tons, and known as St. Patrick's Ball, or Arrow.

Far away, some twenty or more miles to the north, is the lofty range of Slieve-Bloom mountains, in a prominent peak in the southern part of which is a large and very noticeable indentation, supposed to correspond somewhat in outline with the rock at Cashel. This peak is called 'The Devil's Bit, or Bite' Mountain. The legend is briefly this: The devil on one occasion in these mountains met with St. Patrick, and, being worsted in a controversy into which he entered with him, at his departing he seized with his teeth in his rage a large portion of the mountain ridge, and bore it away with him across the rich country to the south, in his mouth. The saint, thus becoming aware who his visitor was, seized another and smaller piece of rock in his hand, and hurled it after his infernal majesty, and, striking him therewith, caused him to drop the mass of rock on the rich plain of Tipperary, where it now constitutes the famous Rock of Cashel; while the saint's bolt also remains where it fell, when it had executed its mission, at the foot of its larger companion.

SITES OF CHURCHES.

A very common legend refers to the endeavours of Satan to prevent churches from being erected upon sites objectionable to him.

The legend is found, with slight variations, in many Yorkshire parishes.

Near Thornton-le-Moor, in the parish of North Otterington, there is a slight eminence, on which, in all probability, stood at one time an ancient village—though no trace of either the village or its name now remains—except the designation of the adjoining fields as 'the Tofts,' and the socket of an old cross known by the degenerate name of 'Perry Trough.'

At this place, says legend, the parish church was to have been erected. The stones were brought to the spot, and the foundations laid, but during the night they were torn up, and by invisible hands borne away for more than a mile across the country to North Otterington. Several times were they brought back to the site during the daytime, but as often were they again removed in the night. At last the builders became weary of the process, and erected the church at the place indicated at North Otterington, where for nigh a thousand years it has stood as the old parish church, dedicated to St. Michael.

A considerable portion of the building now standing is late Norman, or transitional work, of the date about 1120 A.D. Fragments of Saxon crosses have been found built into the masonry.

An exactly similar legend is found in the adjoining parish of Leake, accounting for the present remote situation of the ancient church of that parish. The intention of the builders, it is said, was to have erected it on the top of Borrowby Bank, convenient to the populous village of Borrowby, but their intentions were frustrated by the same agency, and in the same manner, as those of the builders of North Otterington Church.

Thumb-Marks on the Haddock.

The two dark marks on the shoulders of the haddock are, by the legends of many lands, attributed to the Evil One; though by another legend the fish is said to have been the one caught by St. Peter, at his Divine Master's command, in the Sea of Galilee, and the marks to have been those of the apostle's finger and thumb, made in holding the fish while he extracted the piece of money for the tribute from its mouth. The Yorkshire legend, however, brings the origin of the marks nearer home. According to it, the Devil was the builder of the well-known dangerous ridge of rocks known as Filey Brigg. As he was proceeding with this work, he, by chance, dropped his hammer into the water. Diving, in haste to recover it, he by mistake seized a haddock instead of the hammer. Since then the whole species has borne upon its sides the marks of the infernal hand, and shall so bear them to the end of time.

The Devil's Bridge.

The highway between Pateley Bridge and Grassington crosses, in the parish of Burnsall, the deep dell in which runs the small river Dibb, or Dibble, by a bridge known in legend as the Devil's Bridge. It might reasonably be supposed that Deep-dell Bridge, or Dibble Bridge, was the correct and desirable designation, but legend and local tradition will by no means have it so, and account for the less pleasant name in the following manner.

In the days when Fountain's Abbey was in its prime, a shoemaker and small tenant of part of the Abbey lands, named Ralph Calvert, resided at Thorp-sub-Montem, and journeyed twice a year along this road to pay his rent to the Abbot, dispose of the fruits of his six months' handiwork, and return the shoes entrusted to him on his previous visit for repair, and bring back with him, on his return, a bag well filled with others that needed his attention.

The night before setting out, on one of these occasions, he had a fearful dream, in which he struggled with the devil, who, in this wild, rocky ravine, amid unpleasant surroundings, endeavoured to thrust Ralph into a bag, similar to the one in which he carried his stock-in-trade. This he and his wife feared boded no good. In the morning, however, he started on his journey, and duly reached the abbey, assisted at the service, did his business with the abbot and brethren, and then started, with his well-filled bag, on his return homewards. When he arrived near home, in the deep ravine, where on previous occasions he had found but a small brook which he could easily ford, he now found a mountain torrent, through which he only with difficulty and some danger made his way. Having accomplished the passage, he sat down to rest and to dry his wetted garments. As he sat and contemplated the place, he could not but recall how exactly it corresponded with the spot seen in his dream, and at which the author of evil had tried to bag him. Dwelling on this brought anything but pleasant thoughts, and to drive them away, and to divert his mind, he struck up a familiar song, in which the name of the enemy finds frequent mention, and the refrain of which was:

> 'Sing luck-a-down, heigh down,
> Ho, down derry.'

He was unaware of any presence but his own; but, to his alarm, another voice than his added a further line:

'Tol lol derol, darel dol, dolde derry.'

Ralph thought of his dream. Then he fancied he saw the shadow of a man on the road; then from a projecting corner of a rock he heard a voice reading over a list of delinquents in the neighbourhood, with whom he must remonstrate—Ralph's own name among the rest. Not to be caught eavesdropping Ralph feigned sleep; but after a time was aroused by the stranger, and a long conversation ensued, the upshot of which was, after they had entered into a compact of friendship, that Satan informed the shoemaker who he was, and inquired of the alarmed man if there was anything that he could do for him.

Ralph looked at the swollen torrent, and thought of the danger he had lately incurred in crossing it, and of his future journeys that way to the abbey; and then he said, 'I have heard that you are an able architect; I should wish you to build a bridge across this stream; I know you can do it.'

'Yes,' replied his visitant, 'I can and will do it. At the fourth day from this time, come to this spot and you will be astonished, and you can bring the whole country-side with you, if you like.'

At nightfall Ralph reached his home at Thorpe, and related his adventure to his wife, and added, 'In spite of all that is said against him, the Evil One is an honest gentleman, and I have made him promise to build a bridge at the Gill Ford on the road to Pateley. If he fulfils his promise, St. Crispin bless him.'

The news of Ralph's adventure and of the promise

soon spread among the neighbours, and he had no small amount of village chaff and ridicule to meet before the eventful Saturday—the fourth day—arrived. At last it came. Accompanied by thirty or forty of the villagers, Ralph made his way to the dell, where, on arrival, picture their astonishment at the sight! lo, a beautiful and substantial bridge spanned the abyss! Surveyor, and mason, and priest pronounced it to be perfect. The latter sprinkled it with holy water, caused a cross to be placed at each approach to it, and then declared it to be safe for all Christian people to use. So it remained until the Puritan Minister of Pateley, in the time of the Commonwealth, discerning the story to be a Popish legend, caused the protecting crosses to be removed as idolatrous. After that time, neither the original builder, nor any other person, seems to have thought fit to keep the bridge in 'good and tenantable' repair, and in time it fell into so disreputable and dangerous a condition, that the liberal, and almost magic-working, native of the parish—Sir William Craven, Lord Mayor of London in the reign of the 1st James—took the matter in hand, and built upon the old foundations a more terrestrial, but not less substantial and enduring, structure.

Still men call it the Devil's Bridge.

THE DEVIL'S APRONFUL.

On the high moors, which separate Nidderdale from the heads of the Washburn, Dibble, and other tributaries of the Wharfe, are several remarkable peaks and masses of rock, bearing the names of Nursa Knott, the Apronful of Stones, the Wig Stones (probably meaning, *A. Saxon*, 'War Stones') Pockstones, Grimwith Fell, etc.

The Apronful of Stones is a group of rocks heaped together in delightful confusion, their disorder and name being thus explained:

Once upon a time—whether when he built the bridge over the valley, or at some other time, the record saith not—the Devil was determined to fill up the ravine, or gill, of the Dibble. For this purpose he was carrying these enormous crags in his apron, when, too intent upon his object to properly observe where he placed his feet, he caught with one foot upon the top of Nursa Knott, and, stumbling, the strings of the apron broke, and the contents were thrown upon the ground as they now appear. It is also said of them that if any of them, even now, were to be removed, they would certainly be brought back to their original place during the succeeding night.

Near the Cow and Calf Rocks, at Ilkley, there are two groups of crags rejoicing in the names of 'The Great Apronful' and 'The Little Apronful,' to both of which the like legend attaches.

There are many rocks, as at Almas Cliff, the Chevin, near Otley, the Cow and Calf Rocks, etc., where the weather-worn holes at the top, or possibly, some of them, Druidical excavations, somewhat in the shape of a human foot, are designated the devil's footmarks, with slightly varying legends ascribed to each.

IV.

BARGEST AND GHOST LEGENDS.

'The Pagan's myths through marble lips are spoken,
   And ghosts of old beliefs still flit and moan
 Round fane and altar, overgrown and broken,
   O'er tree-grown barrow and grey ring of stone.'

THE BARGEST OF THE TROLLER'S GILL.

This legend belongs to the same neighbourhood as those of 'The Devil's Bridge' and 'The Devil's Apronful,' viz., to that of the wild gills, or ravines, which intersect the bleak moorlands forming the watershed between the head waters of the tributaries of the Wharfe and the Nidd. Following up one of the streams, which murmur or roar through these ravines, from near the village of Appletreewick, or, as it is locally called, Aptrick, by Skyreholme, for about two miles, a deep fissure through the limestone rock is reached. This is known as the Troller's Gill. A wild, weird, lonely spot, where after heavy rains the torrent rushes for half a mile between masses of rock, sixty or seventy feet high and only a few yards apart. The place has been called the 'Gordale of Appletreewick,' as distinguished from, yet compared with, 'The Gordale of Malham,' and, compared by some for its grandeur and gloom—not to the favour of the latter.

In the whole of this neighbourhood, belief in the bargest, or spectre hound, has held a prominent place in popular superstition and folklore. The usual form assumed by this apparition was (is?) that of a large dog, with long hair, immense eyes, large as saucers and bright as fire. Often he dragged with him, fixed to his feet, or round his neck, a chain, whose clanking, in the stillness and darkness of night, added much to the terror which he inspired. Many are the places which he 'haunted,' and many are the legends of his appearance; but one of his favourite spots was the dark Troller's Gill, and the following poetical version of the legend of his appearance there, to a dare-devil son of the neighbourhood, is given by the late Dr. Dixon in his 'Stories of Craven Dales,' and is probably from his own pen:

'On the steep fell's crest did the moonlight rest,
    The beams illumined the dale;
And a silvery sheen clothed the forest green,
    As it swayed to the moaning gale.

'From Burnsall's tower the midnight hour
    Had tolled; and all was still,
Save the music sweet, to the tiny feet
Of the elfin band, from the fairy land,
    That tripped on the rounded hill.

'From his cot he stepped, while the household slept,
    And he caroll'd with boisterous glee;
But he no hied to the green hill side
    The fairy train to see.

'He went not to stray with his own dear May
   Along by a pine-clad scar :
And loving gaze on the dazzling rays
   That shot from the Polar-star.

'On what intent is the Troller bent?
   And where is the Troller bound?
To the horrid gill of the eerie hill,
   To call on the Spectre Hound.

'And on did he pass, o'er the dew-bent grass,
   While the sweetest perfumes fell
From myriad flowers, where forest bowers
   O'ershadow that fairy dell.

'And before his eyes did the dark gill rise,
   No moon-ray pierc'd its gloom ;
And his steps around, did the waters sound,
   Like a voice from a haunted tomb.

'And there as he stept, a shuddering crept
   O'er his frame, scarce known to fear,
For he once did deem the sprite of the stream
   Had loudly called "*Forbear !*"

'An aged yew in the rough cliffs grew,
   And under its sombre shade,
Did the Troller rest, while with charms unblest,
   He a magic circle made.

'Then thrice did he turn, where the streamers burn,
   And thrice did he kiss the ground ;
And with solemn tone in that gill so lone,
   He called on the Spectre Hound.

'And a whirlwind swept by and stormy grew the sky,
   While the torrent louder roared ;
And a lurid flame o'er the Troller's stalwart frame
   From each cleft of the gill was poured.

'And a dreadful thing from the cliff did spring;
   Its wild bark thrilled around;
And a fiendish glow flashed forth I trow,
   From the eyes of the Spectre Hound.

. . . .

'When on Barden's height glowed the mountain light,
   And borne on the mountain air,
The priory bell did the peasants tell,
   'Twas the hour of the matin prayer.

'By shepherd men, where the lurid glen
   Doth its rugged jaws expand,
A corse was found, where a dark yew frown'd,
And marks were imprest on the dead man's breast,
   But they seemed not by mortal hand.

. . . .

'In the evening calm a funeral psalm
   Slowly stole o'er the woodland scene;
The hare-bells wave o'er a new-made grave
   In Burnsall's churchyard green.

'That funeral psalm in the evening calm,
   Which echo'd the dell around,
Was his dirge o'er whose grave blue hare-bells wave,
   Who call'd on the Spectre Hound.'

THE BARGEST, NEAR GRASSINGTON.

'His blood did freeze, his brain did burn,
'Twas feared his mind would ne'er return;
   For he was speechless, ghastly, wan,
   Like him of whom the story ran,
   Who spoke the spectre-hound in Man.'
            —*Lay of the Last Minstrel.*

Mr. Joseph Lucas, F.G.S., in his 'Studies in Nidderdale,' quotes the following racy account, as by 'F. W.

J.,' in the *Leeds Mercury Supplement*, February 28th, 1881, of an adventure with this apparition:

'Of this mysterious personage (Bargest) I am able to give a very particular account, having, only a few days ago, seen Billy B——y, who had a full view of it.

'You see, sir,' said Billy, ' as how I'd been a-clock-dressing at Gerston (Grassington), an' I'd stayed raither lat, an' may-be gitten a lile sup o' spirit, but I war far from bein' drunk, an' knaw'd everything 't pass'd. It war about eleven o'clock when I left, an' war at back end o' t' year; an' it war a grand neet. T' mooin war varra breet, an' I nivver seed Rylston Fell plainer i' a' my life. Now, yo' see, sir, I war passin' down t' mill loin, an' I heerd summut cum past me, brush, brush, brush, wi' chains rattlin' a' t' while; but I seed nowt; an' thowt I to mysen', now, this is a most mortal queer thing. An' I then stuid still, an' luik'd about me, but I seed nowt at a', nobbut t' two stane walls on each side o' t' mill loin. Then I heerd again this brush, brush, brush wi' t' chains; for, yo' see, when I stuid still it stopp'd; an' then, thowt I, this mun be a Bargest, 'at sae mitch is said about; an' I hurried on toward t' wood brig, for they say as how this Bargest cannot cross a watter; but, lord, sir, when I gat ow'r t' brig, I heerd this same thing again; so it wud oither hev cross'd t' watter, or gane round by t' spring head (only thirty miles!). An' then I becom' a valiant man, for I war a bit freeten'ed afore; an', thinks I, I'll turn an' hev a peep at this thing. So I went up Greet Bank towards Linton, an' heerd this brush, brush, brush wi' t' chains a' t' way, but I seed nowt; then it stopp'd a' of a sudden. So I turn'd back to gan hame, but I'd hardly reich'd t' door when I heerd again this brush, brush, brush, an' t' chains, going down towards t' Holin House, an' I follow'd it, an' t' mooin then shone varra breet, an' I *seed it tail!* Then, thowt I, thou owd thing! I can say I've seen the' now, so I'll away hame. When I gat to t' door there wor a girt thing like a sheep, but it war bigger, liggin' across t' threshold o' t' door, an' it war woolly like; an', says I, "Git up," an' it wouldn' git up; then, says I, "Stir thysel'!" an' it wouldn't stir itsel'. An' I grew valiant, an' rais'd t' stick to baste it up, an' then it luiked at me, an' sich oies (eyes)! they did glower! an' war as big as saucers, an' like a cruell'd ball; first there war a red ring, then a blue one, then a white one; an' these rings grew less an' less, *till they cum to a dot!* Now, I war nane fear'd on it, tho' it grinned at me fearfully; an' I kept on sayin', "Git up an' stir thysel';" an' t' wife heeard as how I were at t' door, an' she cum to oppen it, an' then this thing gat up an' walk'd off, *for it war more fear'd o' t' wife than it war o' me!* An' I call'd wife, an' she said it war t' Bargest, but ah've nivver seed it since; an' that's a true story.'

The Bosky Dike Boggart.

Near Fewston, in the Forest of Knaresborough, is a spot named Busky or Bosky Dike—no doubt from the bushes, locally called 'busks' or 'bosks,' with which the sides of the narrow gill, through which the brook or dyke runs, were at one time covered. The place has now been denuded of its bosky appendages, and has at present no trace of the former dark and gloomy character which made it the haunt of the *bargest*, or boggart. Often was he seen, in days of old, promenading, with noiseless step, in the shade of the bushes and hedges, his long hair hanging from his sides, and his horrible eyes glaring upon the terrified wayfarer, and dragging with him his fabled chain. When pursued, he almost invariably disappeared at one particular place, where a large drain crosses the road. Of late years he has, however, never been seen. With the darkness of his haunt he has disappeared here, as elsewhere. A village schoolroom was built in 1878 at the place; and with the following *jeu d'esprit* these notices of Bargest legends, which might be extended to almost any length, shall close :

> The Bosky Dyke, the Bosky Dyke,
>   Ah! tread its path with care;
> With silent step haste through its shade,
>   For 'Bargest' wanders there!
> Since days when ev'ry wood and hill
>   By Pan or Bel was crowned;
> And ev'ry river, brook, and copse
>   Some heathen goddess owned,
> Since bright the Druid's altar blazed,
>   And lurid shadows shed,
> On Almus Cliff and Brandrith Rocks,
>   Where human victims bled,
> Hag-witches oft, 'neath Bestham oaks,
>   Have secret revels kept;
> And fairies danced in Clifton Field,
>   When men unconscious slept.
> Dark sprite and ghost of every form,
>   No man e'er saw the like,
> Have played their pranks at midnight hours
>   In haunted Busky Dyke.

There milk-white cats, with eyes of fire,
    Have guarded stile and gate;
And calves and dogs of wondrous shape
    Have met the trav'ller late.

And 'Pad-foot' oft, in shaggy dress,
    With many a clanking chain,
Before the astonished rustic's eyes
    Has vanished in the drain.

On winter's eve, by bright wood fire,
    As winter winds do roar,
And heap the snow on casement higher,
    Or beat against the door;

Long tales are told from sire to son,
    In many a forest ingle,
Of rushing sounds and fearful sights
    In Busky Dyke's dark dingle.

But lo! there now, as deftly reared,
    As if by magic wands,
In superstition's own domain,
    A village schoolroom stands.

Where thickest fell the gloom of night,
    And terror held its sway,
Now beams the rising sun of light,
    And intellectual day.

Before its beams, its warmth, its power,
    Let every phantom melt,
And children's gambols now be heard
    Where 'fearful bargest' dwelt.

Yet softly tread, with rev'rent step,
    Along the Busky shade;
There ghosts our fathers feared of old
    Will be for ever 'laid.'

The appearance of Bargest a presage of death.

THE WISE WOMAN OF LITTONDALE.

In Hone's 'Table Book' is to be found the following legendary story:

'In the year 17—, in a lonely gill not far from Arncliffe, stood a solitary cottage. A more wretched habitation the imagination cannot picture. It contained a single apartment, inhabited by an old woman called Bertha, who was throughout the valley accounted a wise woman, and a practiser of the "art that none may name." In the autumn, or rather in the latter end of the summer, of 17—, I set out one evening to visit the cottage of the wise woman. I had never beheld the interior, and, led on by curiosity and mischief, was determined to see it. Having arrived at the cottage, I knocked at the gate.

'"Come in," said a voice which I knew to be Bertha's.

'I entered. The old woman was seated on a three-legged stool by a turf fire, surrounded by three black cats and an old sheep-dog.

'"Well," she exclaimed, "what brings you here? What can have induced you to pay a visit to old Bertha?"

'I answered: "Be not offended. I have never before this evening viewed the interior of your cottage, and, wishing to do so, have made this visit. I wished, also, to see you perform some of your *incantations*."

'I pronounced the last word ironically, and Bertha observed it, and said:

'" Then you doubt my power, think me an impostor, and consider my incantations mere jugglery. You *may* think otherwise. But sit down by my humble hearth, and in less than half an hour you shall see such an instance of my power as I have never hitherto allowed mortal to witness."

'I obeyed, and approached the fire. I now gazed around me, and minutely viewed the apartment. Three stools, an old deal table and a few pans, three pictures of Merlin, Nostradamus, and Michael Scott, a cauldron and a sack, with the contents of which I was unacquainted, formed the whole stock of Bertha.

'The witch, having sat by me a few minutes, rose and said:

'" Now for our incantations. Behold me, but interrupt me not."

'She then with chalk drew a circle on the floor, and in the midst of it placed a chafing dish filled with burning embers. On this she fixed the cauldron, which she had half filled with water. She then commanded me to take my station at the further end of the circle, which I did accordingly. Bertha then opened the sack, and, taking from it various ingredients, threw them into the " charmed pot." Amongst other articles I noticed a skeleton head, bones of different sizes, and dried carcasses of some small animals. While thus employed she continued muttering some words in an unknown language; all I remember hearing was the word *konig*. At length the water boiled, and the witch, presenting me with a glass, told me to look through it at the cauldron. I did so, and beheld a figure enveloped in the steam. At the first glance I knew not what to make of it; but I soon recognised the face of N——, a friend and intimate acquaintance. He was dressed in his usual mode, but seemed unwell and pale. I was astonished, and trembled. The figure having disappeared, Bertha removed the cauldron and extinguished the fire.

'"Now," said she, "do you doubt my power? I have brought before you the form of a person who is some miles from this place: was there any deception in the appearance? I am no impostor, though you have hitherto regarded me as such."

'She ceased speaking. I hurried to the door, and said, "Good-night, Bertha."

'"Stop," said she; "I have not done with you. I will show you something more wonderful than the appearance of this evening. To-morrow, at midnight, go and stand upon Arncliffe Bridge, and look at the water on the left side of it. Nothing will harm you; fear not."

'"And why should I go to Arncliffe Bridge? What end can be answered by it? The place is lonely; I dread to be there at such an hour. May I have a companion?"

'"No."

'"Why not."

'"Because the charm will be broken."

'"What charm?"

'"I cannot tell."

'"You will not?"

'"I will not give you any further information. Obey me; nothing shall harm you."

'"Well, Bertha," I said, "you shall be obeyed. I believe you would do me no injury. I will repair to Arncliffe Bridge to-morrow at midnight. Good-night."

'I then left the cottage and returned home. When I retired to rest I could not sleep—slumber fled my pillow—and with restless eyes I lay ruminating upon the strange occurrences at the cottage, and on what I was to behold on Arncliffe Bridge. Morning dawned. I arose unrefreshed and fatigued. During the day I was unable to attend to my business; my coming adventure entirely engrossed my mind.

'Night arrived. I repaired to the bridge. Never shall I forget the scene. It was a lovely night. The full-orbed moon was sailing peacefully through a clear blue, cloudless sky, and its beams, like streaks of silvery lustre, were dancing on the waters of the Skirfare; and the moonlight falling on the hills, formed them into a variety of fantastic shapes. Here one might behold the semblance of a ruined abbey, with towers and spires and Anglo-Saxon and Gothic arches; at another place there seemed a castle frowning in feudal grandeur, with its buttresses, battlements, and parapets. The stillness which reigned around, broken only by the murmuring of the stream, the cottages scattered here and there along its banks, and the woods wearing an autumnal tinge, all united to compose a scene of calm and perfect beauty. I leaned against the left battlement of the bridge. I waited a quarter of an hour, half an hour, an hour; nothing appeared. I listened: all was silent. I looked around: I saw nothing.

'"Surely," I inwardly ejaculated, "I have mistaken

the hour! No; it must be midnight. Bertha has deceived me, fool that I am! Why have I obeyed the beldam?"

'Thus I reasoned. The clock of the neighbouring church chimed; I counted the strokes—it was twelve o'clock. I *had* mistaken the hour, and resolved to stay a little longer on the bridge. I resumed my station, which I had quitted, and gazed on the stream. The river in that part runs in a clear, still channel, and all its music dies away. As I looked on the stream I heard a low, moaning sound, and perceived the water violently troubled without any apparent cause. The disturbance having continued a few minutes, ceased, and the river became calm, and again flowed on in peacefulness. What could this mean? Whence came that low, moaning sound? What caused the disturbance of the river? I asked myself these questions again and again, unable to give them any rational answer. With a slight indescribable kind of fear I bent my steps homewards.

'On turning a corner of the lane that led to my father's house, a huge dog, apparently of the Newfoundland breed, crossed my path, and looked wistfully on me.

'"Poor fellow!" I exclaimed, "hast thou lost thy master? Come home with me, and I will use thee well till we find him."

'The dog followed me, and when I arrived at my place of abode I looked for it, but saw no traces of it, and I conjectured it had found its master.

'On the following morning I repaired again to the cottage of the witch, and found her, as on the former occasion, seated by the fire.

'"Well, Bertha," I said, "I have obeyed you. I was yesterday, at midnight, on Arncliffe Bridge."

'"And of what sight were you a witness?"

'"I saw nothing except a slight disturbance of the stream."

'"I know," said she, "that you saw a disturbance of the water; but did you behold nothing more?"

'"Nothing."

'"Nothing! Your memory fails you."

'"I forgot, Bertha. As I was proceeding home I met a Newfoundland dog, which I supposed belonged to some traveller."

'"That dog," answered Bertha, "never belonged to mortal; no human being is his master. The dog you saw was Bargest! You may perhaps have heard of him?"

'"I have frequently heard tales of Bargest, but I never credited them. If the legend of my native hills be true, a death may be expected to follow his appearance."

'"You are right, and a death will follow his last night's appearance."

'"Whose death?"

'"Not yours."

'As Bertha refused to make any further communication, I left her. In less than three hours after I quitted her I was informed that my friend N——, whose figure I had seen enveloped in the mist of the cauldron, had that morning committed suicide by drowning himself at Arncliffe Bridge, in the very spot where I beheld the disturbance of the stream.'

The Ghost at Trinity Church, York.

One of the most curious and, as yet, unexplained illusions, giving us a real ghost in this nineteenth century, is the now well-known apparition or phantom nun of Holy Trinity Church, Micklegate, York.

A very full description of the scene on which it appears, and of the ghost itself, is given in Baring Gould's 'Yorkshire Oddities,' vol. i., to which those readers who are curious, and would learn more with regard to it, are referred.

For the purpose of explaining the legends connected with it, the following descriptions of the apparition, by three observers, may be quoted.

A writer, 'A. B.' writing in 1866, sends to Mr. Baring Gould an account of what he saw from the gallery at the west end of the church:

'The east window of the church, I must explain, is of stained glass. The peculiarity of the apparition is, that it is seen on the window itself, rather less than half-way from the bottom, and has much the same effect as that of a slide drawn through a magic-lantern when seen on the exhibiting-sheet. The form seen, I am told invariably, is that of a figure dressed in white walking across the window, and gives the idea of someone passing in the churchyard in a surplice. I say a figure, for the number is generally limited to one, and I was told that only on Trinity Sunday did more than one appear, and that then there were three. But I can vouch for the larger number appearing on other occasions, as on the day I was there, which was one of the Sundays after Trinity, there were rarely fewer than three visible.

'Of the three figures, two were evidently those of women, and the third was a little child. The two women were very distinct in appearance; one was tall and very graceful, and the other middle-sized. We called the second one the nursemaid, from her evident care of the child during the absence of the mother, which relationship we attributed to the tall one, from the passionate affection she exhibited towards the child, her caressing it, and the wringing of her hands over it. I may add that each figure is perfectly distinct from the other, and after they have been seen once or twice are at once recognisable.

'The order of their proceedings, with slight variations, was this:—The mother came alone from the north side of the window, and having gone half-way across, stopped, turned round, and waved her hand towards the quarter whence she had come. This signal was answered by the entry of the nurse with the child. Both figures then bent over the child and seemed to bemoan its fate; but the taller one was always the most endearing in her gestures. The mother then moved towards the other side of the window, taking the child with her, leaving the nurse in the centre of the window, from which she gradually retired towards the north corner, whence she had come, waving her hand, as though making signs of farewell, as she retreated.

'After some little time she again reappeared, bending forward, and evidently anticipating the return of the other two, who never failed to reappear from the south side of the window, where they had disappeared.

'The same gestures of despair and distress were repeated, and then all three retired together to the north side of the window.

'Usually they appeared during the musical portions of the service, and especially during one long eight-line hymn, when—for the only occasion without the child—the two women rushed on (in stage phrase), and remained during the whole hymn, making the most frantic gestures of despair. Indeed, the louder the music in that hymn, the more carried away with their grief did they seem to be.'

Another correspondent, 'L. S.,' under the date March, 1874, wrote to Mr. Baring Gould:

'I went many times to the gallery in hopes of seeing the phenomenon, but was repeatedly disappointed. At last, one dull day, hopeless for the purpose, as I thought —rain was falling at the time—I was startled by seeing something.

'There are two east windows—one on the right, filled with common green glass, the organ in front of it. From the outside of this window I saw something move, and immediately a graceful figure of a girl of eighteen or twenty years crossed the outside of the stained east window with a light, free step. She was entirely covered with a fine lace veil, which, as she walked and met the air, showed the outline of the head and figure. The features I could not distinguish, but could see a shade through the veil where they naturally would be.

'The veil was of a pure white, flowing back as a

train as she walked. In two or three minutes the figure returned, the robe flowing back in the same way, and disappeared behind the organ-window.'

A writer, 'H. G. F. T.,' quoted in the *Ripon and Richmond Chronicle*, May 6th, 1876, thus gives his observations:

'The seat I occupied (in the gallery, Easter Day, 1876) was not an advantageous one, a large glass chandelier being between me and the lower panes of the window (east). In the middle of the service, my eyes, which had hardly once moved from the left or north side of the window, were attracted by a bright light, formed like a female, robed and hooded, passing from north to south with a rapid, gliding motion, outside the church, apparently at some distance. There are four divisions in the window, all of stained glass, but at the edge of each runs a rim of plain transparent glass, about two inches wide, and adjoining the stonework. Through this rim especially could be seen what looked like a form, transparent, but yet thick (if such a term can be used) with light. It did not resemble linen, for instance, but was far brighter. The robe was long and trailed. It was, of course, not visible when it had crossed the window and passed behind the wall. . . . About half an hour later it again passed across from north to south, and having remained about ten seconds only, returned with what I believe to have been the figure of a young child, and stopped at the last pane but one, and then vanished. I did not see the child again, but a few seconds afterwards the woman reappeared, and completed the passage behind the last pane very rapidly. Nothing more was seen during the service.

'It is said to appear very frequently on Trinity Sunday, and to bring two other figures on to the scene, another female, called the nurse, and the child. It is often seen as distinctly on a dark, rainy, or snowy day, as when the sun is shining. When I saw it the sun was not bright. The motion is even—not at all jerky. Sometimes the figure glides swiftly, at other times slowly.'

It would be marvellous if this illusion had not given rise to many legends accounting for it. One is, that in the disturbed times of the suppression of religious houses, before the Reformation, a party of soldiers came to sack the convent attached to this church. Having broken in the door, they were met by the abbess, a lady of great courage and devotion, who stood in their way of entering, and declared that they should only pass in over her body, and that should they slay her, and succeed in their errand of destruction, her spirit would haunt the place, until the time came that their sacrilegious work was undone by the rebuilding of the holy house.

This legend has been very prettily versified by E. A. Ould, and published in the *Yorkshire Chronicle* a few years ago. Having described the sunset of a summer's evening, he pictures the city sinking into Nature's rest:

> 'Above old Ebor's ramparts the convent walls arise,
> Transplendent and reflecting the glory of the skies;
> The heavenward-pointing crosses the waning lights dismiss,
> And dreamy Ouse returneth the sunset's parting kiss;
> The vesper bells are ringing o'er field, and tree, and dell,
> The warbling lark is singing, to parting day, farewell;

Now wreaths of mist ascending, like holy incense creep,
O'er buttress, hall, and tower, o'er spire and turret steep;
And through its gauzy curtain the stars a vigil keep,
The breezes sigh a lullaby and—Nature is asleep.'

Then we are told of the arrival of the sacrilegious band of soldiers from the south thus:

'On Twilight's cheek the rosy flush
   Had scarcely turned to gray,
When on the quiet air is borne,
   Along the southern way,
The pattering sounds of horses' hoofs
   And clink of coat and mail,
And soon a goodly band of knights
   The Southern Bar assail;
The trappings of their jaded steeds
   Are dim with dust and soil,
And travel-stain and drooping plume
   Their martial splendour spoil;
But tho' the knights are weary, and
   Exhausted is the steed,
They do not stay to rest, but on
   Their mission they proceed;
And soon before the convent gates
   The martial *cortége* stands:
Their leader, thundering at the door,
   An entrance there demands.

. . . .

'The door of iron-studded oak
   With blows is nearly down,
The leader urges on his band
   With many a curse and frown;
For he will hold no parley,
   No errand will explain,
An entrance for King Henry's band,
   An entrance he will gain.

> Like hungry wolves without the fold,
>   Where harmless sheep reside,
> They fight and clamour, when, behold,
>   The door swings open wide!
> And silence falls like that which fills
>   The chamber of the dead,
> And every man falls back amazed,
>   And bares his shaggy head;
> For fearless on the threshold stands
>   A lady all *alone*:
> The tumult in her woman's heart
>   Has turned that heart to stone.'

He then describes the fragile but erect form of the Abbess, barring the way with a firm majesty of mien, and eyes in which there lives a dangerous light—so different to her usual appearance.

> ' For those soft eyes can swim with tears
>   At any tale of woe,
> As oft in pity they have flowed
>   In days not long ago.
>   .   .   .   .
> ' But now the time has come to bid
>   Adieu to woman's heart,
> For kingly tyranny invades
>   God's righteous, chosen part.
> And shall she aid the crying wrong,
>   Shall she to robbers bow?
> "Be brave," has always been her theme,
>   Shall she surrender now?
> No! let the life that God has given
>   Be in His service spent.
> So there she stands, and straight demands
>   Their errand and intent.'

Sir Ralph, the leader, explains that she and the whole

sisterhood must at once be ejected from their house, and demands the keys. The Abbess replies:

> 'Sir Knight, you are an Englishman,
>   I trust a Christian too.
> I seek for mercy at your hands,
>   The feeble woman's due.
> It is not for myself I crave
>   Your courtesy to-night,
> But for my helpless fold of sheep,
>   And for the cause of right.
> By soldier's honour, woman's tears,
>   By every sacred pledge,
> I charge you lay not on your soul
>   The crime of sacrilege.
> What! are my prayers of no avail?
>   You bid your men proceed?
> Come, cowards, then! who crush the weak—
>   God help us in our need!—
> Come, and this feeble arm of mine
>   Your progress shall restrain;
> Come, and this heart shall cease to beat
>   Ere you an entrance gain;
> Come, then, and if with murderous hand
>   You set my spirit free,
> It will not leave you to enjoy
>   Your blood-bought victory;
> For it will haunt its convent home,
>   Which God has ever blessed,
> But now shall curse, nor suffer here
>   The heretic to rest;
> And ever shall my form appear
>   As witness of this deed,
> To brand your name with infamy,
>   So, if you dare—proceed!'

Sir Ralph then laughed a hideous laugh, unsheathed

his blade, and cried, with dreadful oath and shameless jest:

'" Mad woman, turn aside!"
 The lady stood as still as was
The virgin's image white.
 "Stand back!" the ruffian cried again,
And clouds obscured the light.
 And then the nuns in terror fled,
And on the threshold stone
 One figure stood, like angel good,
Amid the fiends—*alone.*
 "Stand back, or die!" he cried again,
The band advanced a pace,
 She raised aloft her snowy arm,
And turned to heaven her face.
 A pause—the word "Advance" is given—
A rush, a muffled tread—
 A weary sigh—the moon on high—
A holy woman—*dead;*
 A throng of scared and shrieking nuns—
A band of ruthless men—
 A furious mob without, and yells
Of execration—then
 A struggle fierce, and flames that burst
On high with lurid light.
 These were the sounds that met the ear,
 These were the scenes that froze with fear,
Upon that fatal night.

. . . .

' Those days have passed and perished,
 Three centuries have fled
Since in that stony portal gate
 The martyred nun lay dead.

' Her name is now forgotten,
 Her grave is now unknown;
And reverent tears no more bedew
 Her monumental stone.

'The house she loved is levelled,
  The church has seen decay ;
And other worshippers are found
  Where once she loved to pray.

'But faithful to her promise,
  Thro' all these changing years,
Within those sacred precincts still
  The Phantom Nun appears.

. . . . . .

'A little form appeareth,
  And passeth to and fro ;
And those who see remember how,
  Three centuries ago,

'Against the power of tyrants
  A noble woman fought ;
And fighting, died, and with her blood
  A martyr's glory bought.

'Still in the Church's service
  She strives, and never rests ;
For there her shadowy form against
  Usurping power protests.

'But when once more the Convent
  O'er Ebor's walls shall rise,
And matin-song and vesper-bell
  Shall echo to the skies—

'(So says the ancient legend)
  Her work will then be done,
And in her honoured grave at last
  Shall sleep the Phantom Nun.'

Another and very different legend accounts for the appearance—not of one woman only, and that a nun—but of three figures.

It is thus given by Baring Gould's correspondent 'L. S.':

'The Sunday-school children who sit in the gallery see the forms so often as to be quite familiar with the sight, and call them "the mother, nurse, and child." The legend that I have heard told of it is that a family, consisting of a father, mother, and only child, lived here once upon a time. The father died, and was buried at the east end of the church, under or near the organ-window. After a while the plague broke out in York, and carried off the child, and it was buried outside the city, as those who died of plague were not allowed to be laid in the churchyards for fear of communicating the infection. The mother died afterwards, and was laid in her husband's grave, and now, as in her lifetime, continues to visit the grave of her child and bemoan the separation. The child is brought from its grave in the plague-pit by the mother and nurse, and brought to the grave of its father, and then it is taken back to where it lies outside the walls.'

V.
LEGENDS AND TRADITIONS OF MOTHER SHIPTON.

'O yes! If any man or woman, in city, town, or country, can tell any tydings of Agatha Shipton, the daughter of Solomon Shipton, ditch digger, lately deceased, let them bring word to the cryer of the village, and they shall be well rewarded for their pains.'—*A Comedy*, 1660 A.D.

FEW names of Yorkshire celebrities have gained more wide notoriety than that of Mother Shipton. It may be taken as tolerably certain that such a person was born in the neighbourhood of Knaresborough, and lived at the period assigned to her. The legends with regard to her may be divided into two parts—(1) Those which give the marvels of her birth, childhood, and life; (2) Those which relate to her prophecies.

The most marvellous stories of her parentage and life appear in a book by Richard Head, gentleman, published in 1684 A.D., that is, 130 years after the date usually given of the notorious woman's death. He states that he obtained them from an ancient manuscript handed to him by a gentleman, who had it from one of the dissolved monasteries; but the statement is no doubt fictitious.

The stories may have, some of them, lingered in the neighbourhood, handed down through three or four generations, and have been gathered up and woven together by Richard Head; but far more probably they are creations of his own brain. However this may be, the following are a few of them.

The story of her infernal parentage we pass over. Her mother Agatha died in giving her birth. Such strange and horrible noises attended her entry into the world, that the persons present were sorely tempted to fly from the place. The future hag was as ill-favoured in her infancy as in her old age. At any rate she could scarcely have been more repulsive at the end than she was at the beginning.

'According to the best observation of her,' says the writer, 'take this true but not full account of her features and body :—

'She was of an indifferent height, but very morose and big bon'd, her head very long, with very great goggling but sharp and fiery eyes; her nose of an incredible and improportionable length, having in it many crooks and turnings, adorned with many strange pimples of divers colors, as red, blue, and mix't, which like vapors of brimstone, gave such a lustre to her affrighted spectators in the dead-time of the night, that one of them confessed several times, in my hearing, that her nurse needed no other light to assist her in the performance of her duty. Her cheeks were of a black, swarthy complexion, much like a mixture of black and yellow jaundices, wrinkled, shrivelled, and very hollow; insomuch, that as the ribs of her body, so the impressions of her teeth, were easily to be discerned through both sides of her face, answering one side to the other, like the notches in a valley, excepting only two of them, which stood quite out of her mouth, in imitation of the tuskes of a wild boar, or the tooth of an elephant. . . . The neck was so strangely distorted that her right shoulder was forced to be a supporter to her head, it being prop't up by the help of her chin. . . . . Her legs were crooked and misshapen. The toes of her feet looking towards her left side, so that it was very hard for any person (could she have stood up) to guess which road she intended to steer her course, because she never could look that way she resolved to go.'

In due time the infant was put out to nurse, by the parish, to a poor woman near the town. One day when the child had been with her about six months, the woman left the house for a short time, closing the door after her, and leaving the child within alone. When she returned she found the door open, and called some of her neighbours to her assistance, thinking that thieves were within. When they approached the door, and were about to enter, they were startled by a noise in the inner room like a concert of cats, which so affrighted them, that those who had got in endeavoured to get out again quicker than they entered. But in vain, for great long yokes, in the form of a cross, were put round their necks, so that they could not possibly flee out. At last, after much struggling and crying out, the yokes fell off, but in their stead a staff was laid across their shoulders, upon which an old woman appeared, sometimes hanging from it by her heels, and sometimes by her toes. These antics went on for about half an hour, so that the poor men were never more tired, and never more pleased, than when they were allowed to escape from the house. The women did not fare so well. In an inner room they were compelled to take hold of the four ends of a cross and dance round, one after another, until nearly wearied to death; an imp, in the shape of a monkey, hanging on to each, and goading them on with pins whenever they flagged in the exercise. At length they, too, were allowed to escape. The occurrence set the whole town in an uproar. The priest and leading inhabitants consulted as to what was to be done. At length they resolved to go to the house; but as they came near a dissension arose as to who should enter first. It was settled by the priest being put first, and, closely followed by those who should accompany him, with the greatest trepidation—quivering and shaking—they crossed the threshold; but no sooner had they done so, though the floor of the house was only an earthen one, than there was a noise as of a number of men walking over a quantity of stones; then very sweet musical notes were heard, but no one knew whence they came. Out rushed parson and people pell-mell together. Gathering courage, they again entered, and searching the house, missed the child. After examining every corner, one of them looked up the chimney; and there, behold, was the child and cradle, hanging without any support, about three yards from the ground. They contrived to get them both down, and encouraging the poor nurse-woman not to be affrighted, they left the house themselves, no wiser than when they entered it.

As the child grew up, the woman's troubles continued. The greater part of her daily work was to put right in her house what was, in most mysterious ways, continually going wrong. The chairs and stools would frequently march upstairs and down, play at bowls with trenchers and dishes; sometimes at dinner the meat would be spirited away before she could secure a bite. These things seemed greatly to please the future 'Mother Shipton,' who, with one of her monstrous smiles, usually pacified the nurse with the words: 'Be contented, there is nothing here that will harm you.'

The growing Ursula was next sent to school. 'There,' in the words of the imaginative chronicler, 'her mistress began to instruct her, as other children, beginning with the *cris-cross-row*, as they called it, showing and naming only three or four letters at first, but, to the amazement and astonishment of her mistress, she exactly pronounced every letter in the alphabet without teaching. Hereupon her mistress showed her a primer, which she read as well at first sight as any in the school, and so proceeded in any book that was showed her.' At the age of twenty-four years she was courted, and soon after married, by one Toby Shipton, of Shipton, near York, and probably went to live with her husband there, and afterwards at Dringhouses and other places in the vicinity.

A biographer of the last century (S. Baker) gives a better account of her than is to be gathered from the aforegoing legends, but his picture of her personal appearance is by no means such as to show what charms won honest Toby for her husband. 'She was born,' says he, 'at Knaresborough, and baptized by the Abbot of Beverley by the name of Ursula Southeil. Her stature was larger than common, her body crooked, her face frightful, but her understanding extraordinary.'

She after this began to grow famous as a fortune-teller, and for the predictions which she uttered, of which more anon.

Old age in time grew even upon Mother Shipton. A long time before her death she foretold the day and the hour. As the time approached she took a solemn leave of her admirers and friends, and then, when the time was come, laid quietly down on her bed and departed, 1561 A.D., in the seventy-sixth year of her age.

A stone monument is said to have been erected to her memory, by the side of the great North Road, between Clifton and Shipton, near York, on which she was represented as a woman upon her knees, with her hands closed before her, in the attitude of prayer; and this epitaph inscribed to her memory:

> 'Here lyes she who never ly'd,
> Whose skill often has been try'd;
> Her prophecies shall still survive,
> And ever keep her name alive.'

This monument is unfortunately, or fortunately, as much a myth as many of the stories of her life. 'The much mutilated sculptured stone,' says a recent writer, 'was the figure of a warrior in armour, which had been a recumbent monumental statue. It was probably brought from the neighbouring abbey of St. Mary, and placed upright as a boundary stone. It has been removed to the museum of the Yorkshire Philosophical Society.'

MOTHER SHIPTON'S PROPHECIES.

> 'Of all the pretty pantomimes,
> That have been seen or sung in rhime,
> Since famous Johnny Rich's times,
>   There's none like Mother Shipton.

>   She pleases folks of every class,
>   She makes her swans and ducklings pass;
>   She shows her hog, she shows her ass,
>   Oh, charming Mother Shipton!
>
> ' Near to the famous dropping well,
>   She first drew breath, as records tell,
>   And had good beer and ale to sell,
>   As ever tongue was tipt on;
>   Her dropping well itself is seen,
>   Quaint goblins hobble round their queen,
>   And little fairies tread the green,
>   Call'd forth by Mother Shipton.'
>
> Song, 1770 A.D.

The reputed prophecies of this ancient Sybil are numerous, and there is this peculiarity with regard to them, that their number and variety seem to be ever increasing. Whatever unusual event or extraordinary occurrence takes place in the vicinity in which she resided, it is certain to be discovered by some person that Mother Shipton had predicted it. The prediction is unheard of and unknown, except to the inner consciousness of some ardent disciple of the prophetess, until the event has fulfilled it, and then up it springs into life and publicity, to the credulity and amazement of whoever will receive it.

The earliest collection of the 'prophecies' extant was printed in 1641 A.D., that is, accepting 1561 A.D. as the date of her death, about eighty years after the latest of them could have been uttered.

There is another edition in 1645 A.D., but the two differ little, and it may be taken for tolerably certain that these books contain a collection of all the wise sayings and dark speeches of Mother Shipton, known eighty years after her death, and that, therefore, any not among these must be regarded as almost certainly of other parentage than that of this ancient mother, and as at least thrice legendary.

The predictions—ancient and modern—of this wonderful woman have lately been thoroughly investigated by W. H. Harrison, who, in an admirable little book, to which I am deeply indebted, has published many of them, and his conclusions with regard to them. As the copy of the original 'prophecies'—edition 1641 A.D.—is not voluminous, it is here given, the spelling being modernized.

THE PROPHECY OF MOTHER SHIPTON IN THE REIGN OF KING HENRY VIII.

When she heard King Henry VIII. should be King, and Cardinal Wolsey should be at York, she said that Cardinal Wolsey should never come to York with the King; and the Cardinal hearing, being angry, sent the Duke of Suffolk, the Lord Percy, and the Lord Darcy to her, who came with their men disguised to the King's house, near York, where, leaving their men, they went to Master Besley at York, and desired him to go with them to Mother Shipton's house, where, when they came, they knocked at the door. She said: 'Come in, Master Besley, and those honourable lords with you.'

Master Besley would have put in the lords before him, but she said: 'Come in, Master Besley; you know the way, but they do not.'

This they thought strange, that she should know them, and never saw them; and then they went into the house, where there was a great fire, and she bade them welcome, calling them all by their names, and sent for some cakes and ale, and they drank and were very merry.

'Mother Shipton,' said the Duke, 'if you knew what we come about, you would not make us so welcome.'

She said the messenger should not be hanged.

'Mother Shipton,' said the Duke, 'you said the Cardinal should never see York.'

'Yea,' said she; 'I said he might see York, but never come at it.'

'But,' said the Duke, 'when he comes to York thou shalt be burned.'

'We shall see that,' said she; and plucking her handkerchief off her head, she threw it into the fire, and it would not burn. Then she took it and put it on again.

'Now,' said the Duke, 'what mean you by this?'

'If this had burned,' said she, 'I might have burned.'

'Mother Shipton,' quoth the Duke, 'what think you of me?'

'My love,' said she, 'the time will come when you will be as low as I am, and that's a low one, indeed.'

My Lord Percy said: 'What say you of me?'

'My lord,' said she, 'shoe your horse in the quick, and you shall do well; but your body will be buried in York pavement, and your head shall be stolen from the bar and carried into France.'

Then said Lord Darcy: 'And what think you of me?'

She said: 'You have made a great gun; shoot it off,

for it will do you no good. You are going to war. You will pain many a man, but you will kill none.'

So they went away.

Not long after the Cardinal came to Cawood, and going to the top of the tower, he asked where York was, and how far it was thither, and said that one had said he should never see York.

'Nay,' said one, 'she said you might see York, but never come at it.'

He vowed to burn her when he came to York. Then they showed him York, and told him it was but eight miles thence. He said he would soon be there; but, being sent for by the King, he died on the way to London, at Leicester, of a laske. And Shipton's wife said to Master Besley: 'Yonder is a fine stall built for the Cardinal in the Minster of gold, pearl, and precious stones. Go, and present one of the pillars to King Henry.' And he did so.

Master Besley, seeing these things fall out as she had foretold, desired her to tell him some more of her prophecies.

'Master,' said she, 'before that Ouse Bridge and Trinity Church meet, they shall build on the day and it shall fall in the night, until they get the highest stone of Trinity Church, to be the lowest stone of Ouse Bridge, then the day shall come when the north shall rue it wondrous sore, but the south shall rue it for evermore.

'When hares kindle on cold hearth-stones, and lads shall marry ladies, and bring them home, then shall you have a year of pining hunger, and then a dearth without corn.

'A woeful day shall be seen in England, a king and queen, the first coming of the King of Scots, shall be at Holgate Town, but he shall not come through the bar; and when the king of the north shall be at London Bridge, his tail shall be at Edinburgh.

'After this shall water come over Ouse bridge, and a windmill shall be set on a tower, and an elm-tree shall lie at every man's door. At that time women shall wear great hats and great bands, and when there is a Lord Mayor at York let him beware of a stab.

'When two knights shall fall out in the castle yard, they shall never be kindly all their lives after. When Colton Hagge hath borne seven years' crops of corn, seven years after you hear news, there shall two judges go in and out at Mungate (Monkgate) Bar.

> 'Then wars shall begin in the spring,
> Much woe to England it shall bring;
> Then shall the ladies cry, Well away,
> That ever we lived to see this day!

Then best for them that have the least, and worst for them that have the most. You shall not know of the war over-night, yet you shall have it in the morning; and when it comes it shall last three years.

> 'Between Cadron [Calder] and Aire
> Shall be great warfare;
> When all the world is as lost,
> It shall be called Christ's crost.

When the battle begins it shall be where crooked-back'd Richard made his fray. They shall say:

> 'To warfare for your King,
> For half a crown a day;
> But stir not, she will say,

>To warfare for your King
>On pain of hanging.
>But stir not, for he that goes to complain,
>Shall not come back again.

'The time will come when England shall tremble and quake for fear of a dead man that shall be heard to speak; then will the Dragon give the Bull a great snap, and when the one is down, they will go to London town.

'Then there will be a great battle between England and Scotland, and they shall be pacified for a time. And when they come to *Brammammore* (? Bramham Moor), they fight, and are again pacified for a time.

'Then there will be a great battle at *Knavesmore*, and they will be pacified for a while.

'Then there will be a great battle between England and Scotland at *Stoknmore* (? Stockton Moor); then will ravens sit on the Cross, and drink as much blood of the nobles as of the commons. Then woe is me, for London shall be destroyed for ever after.

'Then there shall come a woman with one eye, and she shall tread in many men's blood to the knee, and a man leaning on a staff by her; and she shall say to him, "Who art thou?" and he shall say, "I am the King of the Scots." And she shall say, "Go with me to my house, for there are three knights;" and he will go with her, and stay there three days and three nights. Then will England be lost; and they will cry twice of a day, "England is lost!"

'Then there will be three knights in Petergate, in York, and the one shall not know of the other. There shall be a child born in Pomfret with three thumbs, and those three knights will give him three horses to hold while they win England; and all the noble blood shall be gone but one, and they shall carry him to Sheriff Hutton Castle, six miles from York, and he shall die there, and they shall choose there an earl in the field, and, hanging their horses on a thorn, rue the time that ever they were born, to see so much bloodshed.

'Then they will come to York to besiege it, and they shall keep out three days and three nights, and a penny loaf shall be within the bar at half-a-crown, and without the bar at a penny. And they will swear if they will not yield to blow up the town walls. Then they will let them in, and they will hang up the mayor, sheriffs, and aldermen, and they will go into Crouch Church: there will be three knights go in, and but one come out again; and he will cause proclamation to be made, that any man may take house, tower, or bower, for twenty-one years, and whilst the world endurest there shall never be warfare again, nor any more kings or queens, but the kingdom shall be governed by the Lords, and then York shall be London.

'And after this shall be a white harvest of corn gotten in by women. Then shall be in the north that one woman shall say unto another, "Mother, I have seen a man to-day." And for one man there shall be a thousand women. There shall be a man sitting upon St. James's Church Hill weeping his fill.

'And after that a ship shall come sailing up the Thames till it come against London, and the master of the ship shall weep, and the mariners shall ask him why he weepeth, seeing he hath made so good a voyage;

and he shall say, "Ah! what a goodly city this was, none in the world comparable to it, and now there is scarce left any house that can let us have drink for our money."

'Unhappy he that lives to see these days,
But happy are the dead, Shipton's wife says.'

These are the whole of the prophecies that are given by the writer, whose book was printed in 1641 A.D. And it is remarkable that the next edition, of 1645 A.D., not only contains the same, but also the fulfilment of them all, except the one about England quaking for fear of a dead man, and the last one, about the destruction of London, which is, however, said to have been fulfilled by the plague of 1666 A.D., though the time, yet future, of Macaulay's famous New Zealander, sitting on the ruins of London Bridge, seems to accord better with the oracle.

APOCRYPHAL SAYINGS.

A few of the very apocryphal and legendary sayings of Mother Shipton may be mentioned. One,

'When carriages without horses run,
Old England shall be quite undone,'

was never heard of until railways had been introduced and become common in the country. Another one,

'The village of Fewston shall down the Washburn go,'

was discovered among the previously unnoticed prophecies of Mrs. Shipton, when, a few years ago, after the making by the Leeds Corporation of reservoirs in the Washburn Valley, a landslip took place on the hillside, and a portion of the ancient village was thereby reduced to ruins.

'The bridge across the Nidd shall tumble down twice, and on third building stand for ever,' was a prophecy remembered by some ardent admirers of the prophetess, as one of her many sayings, after the railway viaduct at Knaresborough, over the river, had twice fallen, and a third time been rebuilt in 1848.

But the one which has added most, in late years, to the ancient mother's fame, is the following, headed: 'An Ancient Prediction, entitled, by popular tradition, Mother Shipton's Prophecy. Published in 1448, republished in 1641'.:

> 'Carriages without horses shall go,
> And accidents fill the world with woe;
> Around the world thoughts shall fly
> In the twinkling of an eye.
>
> 'The world upside down shall be,
> And gold be found at the root of a tree.
> Through hills man shall ride,
> And no horse be at his side.
>
> 'Under water men shall walk,
> Shall ride, shall sleep, shall talk.
> In the air men shall be seen
> In white, in black, in green.
>
> 'Iron in the water shall float
> As easily as a wooden boat.
> Gold shall be found and shown
> In a land that's now not known.
>
> 'Fire and water shall wonders do,
> England shall at last admit a foe.
> The world to an end shall come
> In eighteen-hundred-and-eighty-one.'

Unfortunately for the mother's fame, a few inquiring spirits were sceptical about the authenticity of this prediction. Among other things, the date given as that of its publication, 1448 A.D., did not at all square with the usually accepted date of the supposed authoress's birth, viz., in 1486, or forty years after the prophecy was said to have been published. Consequently a correspondence was started in *Notes and Queries*, in 1872, on the subject, and this resulted in the following note by the editor of that periodical:

'MOTHER SHIPTON'S PROPHECIES. — Mr. Charles Hindley, of Brighton, in a letter to us, has made a clean breast of having fabricated the prophecy (quoted above) with some others, included in his reprint of a cheap book version, published in 1862 A.D.'

Whether the following belongs to this category I know not. It is undoubtedly of the same class, and is nicely, if not delicately, expressed, and corresponds most accurately with what is now to be seen at Harrogate, the site of which was, in Mother Shipton's days, a wild forest table-land, with a boggy, unexplored vale below, unknown to either science or the world:

> 'When lords and ladies stinking water soss,
> High brigs o' stean the Nidd sal cross,
> And a toon be built o' Harrogate Moss.'

Here we take leave of the legendary sibyl and her sayings. Whether she was the remote but direct ancestress of our familiar friend, Mr. Punch, or not (as Mr. Harrison thinks she was), a writer of legend and tradition must leave to sober archæologists and historians to fight out.

VI.

LEGENDS OF DRAGONS AND OTHER SERPENTINE MONSTERS.

SERPENT-WORSHIP was one of the earliest and most prevalent superstitions of the heathen world, and, even where it has long ceased, relics of it survive in popular superstitions and legends.

Such are prevalent in almost all countries, yet in most of the stories there is a great family likeness. The serpent—whether the ordinary one, or the winged dragon, or wyvern—is almost always represented as the terror and devastator of the country around which it dwells, and is either propitiated by offerings or slain by some champion knight, whose services, as the deliverer and benefactor of the neighbourhood, are perpetuated by monumental stone, or celebrated in local song, or both.

TENURE OF THE MANOR OF SOCKBURN.

The river Tees, separating Yorkshire from Durham, is crossed at Croft by one of the principal bridges which connect the two counties.

The owner of the neighbouring manor of Sockburn, held under the bishopric of Durham, is said to be required, by the terms of his feudal tenure, to meet every new bishop of that see upon the centre of this bridge, and there present before him an ancient sword, at the same time repeating these words: 'My Lord Bishop, I here present before you the falchion wherewith the champion Conyers slew the worm-dragon, or fiery flying serpent, which destroyed man, woman, and child, in memory of which the king then reigning gave him the manor of Sockburn to hold by this tenure, that upon the first entrance of every bishop of Durham into the county, this falchion should be presented.' Upon which the bishop is supposed to take the weapon into his hand, and then immediately return it, wishing the Lord of Sockburn health and long enjoyment of his manor.

For the above, and the following five legends, the writer is entirely indebted to a paper, entitled 'Serpent Legends of Yorkshire,' in the *Leisure Hour* for May, 1878.

THE SERPENT OF HANDALE.

Handale is in the parish of Lofthouse-in-Cleveland. A small priory of Benedictine nuns was founded there in 1133 by William, son of Richard de Percy, no remains of which now exist. The situation is truly delightful and picturesque: the sea, only three miles distant, adds variety to the scene, while the profound seclusion of the woods, the deep solitude and repose of the glens, and the quiet and the retirement around, carry back the thoughts to the remote periods when

> 'Their bells were heard at evening swelling clear,
> By pilgrims wandering o'er the heath-clad hills.'

In ancient times these quiet woods were infested by

a huge serpent, possessed of most singular fascinating powers, which used to beguile young damsels from the paths of truth and duty, and afterwards feed on their dainty limbs. At this time there lived in these parts a brave and gallant youth named Scaw, who felt greatly incensed at the ravages which the serpent made among his fair acquaintances, and he determined to destroy the vile monster, or perish in the attempt. Therefore, amid the tears and prayers of his friends and sweethearts, he buckled on his armour, and proceeded to the serpent's cave. Striking the rock with his sword, the reptile immediately issued from his den, breathing fire from his nostrils, and rearing high his crested head to transfix the bold intruder with his poisonous sting. Nothing daunted, the young hero fought bravely, and after a long and severe contest succeeded in killing the monster. Young Scaw forthwith married an earl's daughter found in the cave, and, by his valour, rescued from a cruel death. By this marriage he obtained vast estates. The wood where he slew the serpent is called 'Scaw Wood' to this day, and the stone coffin in which he was buried is yet shown near the site of the priory.

THE WORM OF SEXHOW.

Sexhow is a small hamlet or township in the parish of Rudby, some four miles from the town of Stokesley, in Cleveland. Upon a round knoll at this place a most pestilent dragon, or worm, took up its abode; whence it came, or what was its origin, no one knew. So voracious was its appetite, that it took the milk of nine cows daily to satisfy its cravings; but we have not heard that it required any other kind of food. When not sufficiently fed, the hissing noise it made alarmed all the country round about; and, worse than that, its breath was so strong as to be absolutely poisonous, and those who breathed it died. This state of things was unbearable, and the country was becoming rapidly depopulated. At length the monster's day of doom dawned. A knight, clad in complete armour, passed that way, whose name or country no one knew, and, after a hard fight, he slew the monster, and left it dead upon the hill, and then passed on his way. He came, he fought, he won; and then he went away. The inhabitants of the hamlet of Sexhow took the skin of the monster-worm and suspended it in the church, over the pew belonging to the hamlet of Sexhow, where it long remained a trophy of the knight's victory, and of their own deliverance from the terrible monster.

THE DRAGON OF LOSCHY WOOD.

In the church of Nunnington, in the North Riding of Yorkshire, is an ancient tomb, surmounted by the figure of a knight in armour, in a recumbent posture, the legs crossed, the feet resting against a dog, the hands apparently clasping a heart, but no inscription to determine to whom the monument belongs. The traditional account current in the neighbourhood is that it is the tomb of Peter Loschy, a famous warrior, whose last exploit was killing a huge serpent, or dragon, which infested the country, and had its den on a wooded eminence called Loschy Hill, near East Newton, in the parish of Stonegrave.

The details of the combat, as related by tradition, are as follows:

Having determined to free the country from the pest, the redoubted Peter Loschy had a suit of armour prepared, every part of it being covered with razor-blades set with the edges outwards; and thus defended, armed only with his sword, and accompanied by a faithful dog, he went forth to seek the destroyer, which he quickly found in a thicket on Loschy Hill.

The dragon, glad of another victim, darted upon the armed man, notwithstanding a wound from his sword, and folded itself around his body, intending, no doubt, as it had often done before, to squeeze its victim to death, and afterwards to devour it at leisure; but in this it was disappointed. The razor-blades were keen, and pierced it in every part, and it quickly uncoiled itself again, when, to the great surprise of the knight, as soon as it rolled on the ground its wounds instantly healed, and it was strong and vigorous as ever; and a long and desperate fight ensued between the knight and the serpent, without much advantage to either. At length the sword of the knight severed a large portion of the serpent, which the dog quickly snatched up in his mouth, and ran across the valley with it nearly a mile, and there left it on a hill near Nunnington Church, and immediately returned to the scene of combat, and, snatching up another fragment, cut off in the same manner, conveyed it to the same place, and returned again and again for other fragments until they were all removed, the last portion conveyed being the poisonous head.

The knight, now rejoicing at his victory, stooped to

pat and praise his faithful dog; the latter, overjoyed, looked up and licked the knight's face, when, sad to relate, the poison of the serpent imbibed by the dog was inhaled by the knight, and he fell down dead in the moment of victory, and the dog also died by the side of his master.

The villagers buried the body of the knight in Nunnington Church, and placed a monument over the grave, on which were carved the figures of the knight and his faithful dog, to witness to the truth of the story.

THE SERPENT OF SLINGSBY.

Slingsby, a small parish-town in the North Riding of Yorkshire, is distinguished for three things: the ruins of a castle, a maypole, and the tradition of an enormous serpent. The castle is comparatively modern, but nevertheless a splendid ruin. The maypole, one among the dozen yet remaining in Yorkshire, reminds us of a time for ever passed away. Our business is with the serpent alone. The road through Slingsby from Hovingham to Malton, instead of proceeding in a direct line, to which there is no natural obstacle, made, until lately altered, a singular and awkward bend to the right. This deviation was observed by Roger Dodsworth, the antiquary, and in reply to his inquiries he received the following story:

'The tradition is that between Malton and this town there was some time a serpent, that lived upon prey of passengers, and which this Wyvill and his dog did kill, when he received his death-wound. There is a great hole half a mile from the town, round within, three yards broad and more, where the serpent lay. In which time the street was turned a mile on the south side, which does still show itself if any takes pains to survey it.'

This tradition, written down in 1619 by one of the most painstaking of antiquaries, is current among the villagers to this day, who yet point out the place where the serpent had its den, declaring that the said serpent was a mile in length, and in support of this story point to the effigies of Wyvill and his dog yet remaining in their church. Both Wyvill and his dog perished in the fight or died soon afterwards, and were commemorated by this monument. Dodsworth saw it, and says, when speaking of Slingsby Church: 'There is in the choir a monument cross-legged of one of the Wyvills, at his feet a talbot coursing.'

THE DRAGON OF WANTLEY.

This is sometimes regarded as a legend of this class, but it is really nothing more than humorous satire. It is related in a humorous ballad which Dr. Percy, in his 'Reliques of Antient Poetry,' dates as early as the seventeenth century. Wortley is in South Yorkshire, some six miles from Rotherham, and near to it is Wharncliffe Lodge and Wharncliffe Wood. The local pronunciation of the name is Wantley. In the reign of Elizabeth a dispute arose between Mr. Nicholas Wortley, as lessee, under the rectory of Penistone, of the great tithes, and some of the inhabitants of the neighbourhood. His right seems to have been disputed, and Sir Francis Wortley, his successor, rightly or wrongly, was accused of enforcing payment in a tyrannical and oppressive manner. The whole of the inhabitants rose against his exactions, and determined to find some champion who would take up their cause against this dragon of Wantley, and put an end to his rapacity over their crops, and cattle, and ruined homes.

They found one in a man—probably an attorney—named in the ballad 'More of More Hall.' 'More Hall,' says Hunter, 'stands in a charming valley near the Don, and enjoys a luxuriant view of the rocks and woods of Wharncliffe. It is now (1819) nothing more than a decent farm-house.' Strictly speaking, there could not be a 'More of More Hall' in the reign of Elizabeth, when the contention is said to have occurred, for the male line of that family became extinct in Edward VI.'s reign. At the time referred to, the hall was inhabited by a gentleman of the name of Blount, who, having married an heiress of the elder family, may have been locally designated 'More of More Hall.' If so, he was the champion who went forth to encounter the dragon of Wantley.

The ballad, as well as being a humorous and satirical description of the legal contest which ensued, is evidently also intended as a burlesque upon some of the rules of mediæval chivalry and the doughty deeds of its knights.

The following is the opening stanza:

> 'Old stories tell how Hercules
>   A dragon slew at Lerna,
> With seven heads and fourteen eyes,
>   To see and well discerna;
> But he had a club this dragon to drub,
>   Or he had ne'er done it I warrant ye;
> But More of More Hall, with nothing at all,
>   He slew the dragon of Wantley.'

Then follows a description of the monster:

> 'This dragon had two furious wings,
>   Each one upon each shoulder,
> With a sting in his tail as long as a flail,
>   Which made him bolder and bolder.
> He had long claws, and in his jaws
>   Four and forty teeth of iron:
> With a hide as tough as any buff,
>   Which did him round environ.'

We have next an account of his ravages throughout the whole neighbourhood. In one case it is said,

> 'Devoured he poor children three,
>   That could not with him grapple;
> And at one sup, he ate them up,
>   As one would eat an apple.'

This is supposed to allude to the spoliation of the property of three co-heiresses of a Mr. Bosville, one of Sir F. Wortley's opponents.

> 'All sorts of cattle this dragon did eat.
>   Some say he ate up trees,
> And that the forests sure he would
>   Devour up by degrees;
> For houses and churches were to him geese and turkeys.
>   He ate up all and left none behind
> But some *stones*, dear Jack, that he could not crack
>   Which on the hills you will find.'

The reference to 'some stones' is to a Mr. Lyonel Rowlestone, who was chiefly instrumental in calling in the services of Mr. More, the lawyer.

The dragon's residence was

> 'In Yorkshire, near fair Rotherham,
>   The place I know it well;
> Some two or three miles or thereabouts
>   I vow I cannot tell;

> But there is a hedge just on the hill-edge,
>   And Matthew's house hard by it;
> O there and then was this dragon's den,
>   You could not choose but spy it.
>
> ' Hard by a furious knight there dwelt,
>   Of whom all towns did ring.
>
> . . . .
>
> ' These children, as I told, being eat;
>   Men, women, girls, and boys,
> Sighing and sobbing, came to his lodging,
>   And made a hideous noise;
> " O save us all, More of More Hall,
>   Thou peerless knight of these woods;
> Do but slay this dragon, who won't leave us a rag on,
>   We'll give thee all our goods."
>
> ' " Tut, tut," quoth he, " no goods want I;
>   But I want, I want in sooth,
> A fair maid of sixteen, that's brisk and keen,
>   With smiles about the mouth;
> Hair black as a sloe, skin white as snow,
>   With blushes her cheeks adorning,
> To anoint me o'er-night, ere I go to fight,
>   And to dress me in the morning." '

The knight next proceeded to Sheffield town, and provided himself with the requisite armour, bristling with spikes in every part. Equipped in this he was the admiration of, and a wonder to, all the neighbourhood, who came forth to see him. Moreover,

> ' He frighted all, cats, dogs, and all,
>   Each cow, each horse, and each hog;
> For fear they did flee, for they took him to be
>   Some strange outlandish hedge-hog.'

His first step against the monster was not a very

knightly one. He hid himself in a well, to which the dragon was expected to come to drink :

> 'It is not strength that always wins,
>   For wit doth strength excel,
> Which made our cunning champion
>   Creep down into a well.'

Thence he was able, covertly, to deal the monster a blow on the mouth, which made him cry ' Boh !'

The knight was, however, compelled to come forth from his ambush and stand up in fair fight. The contest is then described:

> '" Your words," quoth the dragon, " I don't understand,"
>   Then to it they fell at all,
> Like two wild boars so fierce, if I may
>   Compare great things with small.
> Two days and a night with this dragon did fight
>   Our champion on the ground ;
> Though their strength it was great, their skill it was neat,
>   They never had one wound.'

At length, however, the dragon gave the champion a blow which 'made him to reel ;' but this he returned with a kick with the spiked toe of his boot, which put an end to the fight and the monster's life.

> '" Murder, murder !" the dragon cried,
>   " Alack, alack, for grief ;
> Had you but miss'd that place you could
>   Have done me no mischief."
> Then his head he shaked, trembled and quaked,
>   And down he laid and cried ;
> First on one knee, then on back tumbled he,
>   So groaned and kicked and died.'

VII.

LEGENDS AND TRADITIONS OF BATTLES AND BATTLE-FIELDS.

IT is impossible to recite the legends and traditions of battles and battle-fields without entering more or less upon the region of more authentic history. The beads and pearls of legend require to be strung together by, at least, a thread of historical facts run through them to make them intelligible, and give them cohesion. This should, however, be done as sparingly as possible; yet often the reader must be left to distinguish for himself between what is a part of the historical string holding them together, and what are legends or fables.

THE WHITE BATTLE OF MYTON.

In 1319 A.D., when the pusillanimous second Edward was besieging Berwick-on-Tweed, the Scots, under the Earl of Murray and Lord James Douglas, endeavoured to cause a diversion by descending, through the north-west, upon Yorkshire, and, carrying havoc and slaughter in their path, they penetrated as far as the gates of York.

William de Melton, the then archbishop, 'a grave and reverend divine,' together with the Bishop of Ely and the Abbot of Selby, who, with a large number of clergy, were on some ecclesiastical occasion then staying in York, determined to oppose the invaders.

They gathered a number of men—in all about 10,000—pressing into their service 'all that could travel'—husbandman, peasant, ecclesiastic, and citizen alike. Under the command of the archbishop and the Bishop of Ely, this 'mixed multitude' issued from the city to seek the enemy.

'They did not proceed in battle array, but walked stealthily through the fields without any uproar, hoping thereby to take the Scots unawares.' But the canny Northmen were not to be caught napping; and the archbishop and his friends—'men more fit to pray for the success of a battle than to fight for it'—found them drawn up 'in Myton Pasture, near to Swale Water,' and prepared to receive them. 'These men are not men of war—they are hunters, and will do no good!' cried the Scots, when they saw their unwarlike approach.

Well, on the eve of St. Matthew's Day (September 30th), 1319, they met. First the Scots feigned retreat over a wooden bridge that then crossed the Swale at that place. Being pursued, they tried the effects of smoke. Setting fire to several hay-stacks, the thick smoke was driven in the face of the English, and so blinded them that they could not see where their enemies were. Allowing them all to get over the bridge, the Scots then swooped down between it and them and so cut off their retreat; then, falling upon the disorderly rabble, they cut them up without mercy, and 3,000 were left dead on the field, of whom 300 were 'white-robed priests.' They who escaped the sword only fled to perish in the Swale, and had not night come on 'scarce one Englishman would have escaped.'

The archbishop and bishop escaped; but the cross-bearer of the former either lost his master's pastoral cross, or hid it, and was then himself slain. It was found by a husbandman, who had been in hiding during the *mêlée*, and, rejoicing in his treasure—a white elephant to him, with which he did not know what to do—he hid it also in his hut among the hay. There it remained some time, until, conscience-stricken, its finder could retain it no longer, so he took it to York, and returned it into the hands of its owner.

The site of the 'hay-stacks,' whose smoke so puzzled the ecclesiastics, is still pointed out, on the west side of the river, by the tradition of the locality. And, on the same authority, it is said that some of the stones, which formed the foundation or piers of the old bridge, were afterwards used in the rebuilding of Myton Church.

From the command of this unfortunate English levy being held by ecclesiastics, and so many of the same being found in its ranks, the battle has been called 'the White Battle,' or, in derision, 'the Chapter of Myton.'

The Battle of Boroughbridge.

This battle took place in the spring of the year 1322. The second Edward was then on the throne, and Hugh de Spencer, his unpopular favourite, had just returned from the banishment enforced by the barons, and was again in the zenith of his influence over the weak king. Thomas, Earl of Lancaster, the king's uncle, and Bohun, Earl of Hereford, raised the standard of revolt against him, with the object of ridding him of the De Spencers. They were joined by many northern noblemen, and among the rest by John de Mowbray, Lord of Kirby Malzeard, Thirsk, and Upsall Castles, and of the broad acres still known as the Vale of Mowbray.

Afraid to meet the king's forces in the Midland counties, the conspirators were retiring before them towards Scotland, when Sir Andrew Harcla, Governor of Carlisle, and Sir Simeon Ward, Sheriff of Yorkshire, hurriedly gathered a force in the north and intercepted them at Boroughbridge.

It is not within our province to write history, or to give a full account of the battle which ensued. We have to do now only with story and tradition.

The bridge that then spanned the Ure was constructed of wood. Bohun, the powerful Earl of Hereford, led on a body of knights and 'mailed chivalry of England' to force the passage of the bridge against the troops of Harcla, who had seized and held it. A soldier of Harcla's force—said to have been a Welshman—hid himself among the timbers of the bridge, and, as Hereford came upon it, he thrust his long spear through an interstice in the beams above him, which, entering under the armour of the earl, so pierced his body that he died on the spot. Several other of the noblemen of the rebel party were slain, or severely wounded, and their army was utterly routed.

A small chapel stood near the spot. To this the Earl of Lancaster fled for sanctuary, and, flinging himself before the altar, he cried, 'Good Lord, I render myself to Thee, and put me into Thy mercy.' It was, however, to no purpose. He was dragged out and carried a prisoner down the Ouse, by way of York, to Pontefract—his own castle. There he was shortly afterwards—in his own hall—brought before Edward II., condemned, and on June 19th in the same year beheaded, on what is still called St. Thomas's Hill, near Pontefract. He is said to have been canonized, and his shrine to have been a popular place of pilgrimage, and the scene of several miracles.

John de Mowbray was also taken a prisoner, and there is little doubt suffered a like fate to his leader.

But tradition tells a somewhat different story as to his end. It relates that he escaped from the battle, and, galloping to the north, hoped to have found refuge in his stronghold on the slope of the Hambleton Hills, Upsall Castle, near Thirsk. He was, however, pursued by a troop of the king's forces, who, overtaking him as he was passing along a lane within sight of Upsall, seized him, converted the nearest fallen tree into a block, struck off his head, and, denuding the body of its rich armour, threw it into the ditch by the lane-side, and hung up the armour, in derision, in a neighbouring oak.

The lane is still named Chop Head Loaning.

The legend or story has been admirably told in verse by Mrs. Susan K. Phillips as follows:

'All day long at Boro'bridge the battle swayed and roared,
Where Lancaster and Hereford unsheathed the rebel sword,

'The Ure came glittering plainward all bright with moorland dews,
But she ran red with gallant blood or ere she met the Ouse.

'For on the gray bridge arches, and by the willowed banks,
Was Hereford's last desperate stand against the Royal ranks.

'And when upon the Welshman's spear poured the life-blood of De Bohun,
His followers melted from the fray as the tides beneath the moon.

'From violated sanctuary Earl Lancaster they tore,
The best and bravest of the North to prison doom they bore.

'Fast galloped John de Mowbray from the field of Boro'bridge,
Fast to where Upsall's massive walls nestle by Boltby Ridge;

'There stanch hearts to the Mowbray would render homage due,
There bold hearts to the Mowbray give refuge close and true.

'But close upon his traces stern Harcla's riders came,
Eager for traitor Mowbray's head, De Spencer's gold to claim.

'All in the darkening Loaning was the brief unequal fight,
And helpless in fierce foemen's hands stood Mowbray's noble knight.

'The jury of the battle day all form, as mercy, lacks;
A fallen ash-tree bole the block, a soldier's sword the axe.

'Among the ferns the headless trunk in rough dishonour flung,
The gilded armour on an oak in mockery they hung,

'To rust in summer showers, in winter storms to sway ;
No more to flash the tourney's star, to lead the tossing fray.

'It was five hundred years ago ; calm flows the bright brown Ure,
Upon her banks the little town stands quiet and secure.

'Who on the bridge at Boro'bridge thinks of that day in March,
When the brave blood of Hereford stained all the dark gray arch?

'The ancient church where Lancaster fled in his last despair,
How few there be who yet can point and say " It once was there !"

'Gone shrine, and oak, and Milan mail ; De Mowbray's haughty race
Have vanished from the land where yet their name marks vale and chase.

'Yet still tradition treasures up the tales of long ago ;
And still when from Black Hambleton the fierce north-easters blow,

'The fearful peasant passing by " Chop Head Loaning " hears
The sough of boughs, and clash of steel, fall on his shrinking ears,

'As on the unseen branches the knightly harness rings
Defiance to the veil that time o'er name and glory flings.'

THE BATTLE OF WAKEFIELD.

On December 24th, 1460 A.D., ' in the ruthless wars of the White and Red,' was fought the Battle of Wakefield Green, at which fell Richard Duke of York; the young Earl of Rutland, in the retreat afterwards, being slain by Black Clifford. The spots at which both fell are still pointed out by tradition. That at which the Duke was slain is close to the old road from Wakefield to Barnsley, about a mile from Wakefield Bridge, in a hollow and somewhat boggy piece of ground. The old historian, Holinshed, relates that when the victors found his body they subjected it to much mockery and insult, crowning the head 'with segges and bulrushes, and in derision cried, "Hail, King without rule! Hail, King without heritage! Hail, Duke and Prince without people!" etc.' And then the order of Queen Margaret was carried out—

> 'Off with his head, and set it on York Gate,
> So York may overlook the town of York.'

The spot where he thus fell, his spirit (says legend) still haunts. Two large willow-trees, said to have been there at the time, are there still.

> 'A headless form, he walks beneath their shade, in
> The very witching time of night
> When churchyards yawn, and hell itself breathes out
> Contagion to the world.'

A common warning among the villagers of the vicinity, to anyone who has to pass the spot at that hour, is, 'Mind t'Duke o' York without his head doesn't git hod o' thee as thou gans by t'willow-tree.'

The story of the death of the Earl of Rutland, second son of the duke, is usually thus given: When the battle was over, Lord Clifford of Skipton was riding toward Sandal Castle to rejoin the Queen (Margaret). He overtook the youth, who had just learned the death of his father, and was being hurried away by his tutor,

Sir Robert Aspall. Clifford seized the young Earl, who fell on his knees and begged for mercy.

'Who is he?' asked Clifford.

'He is the son of a prince who is now beyond thy power,' replied the tutor; 'but I pray you spare him, for he is too young to do you injury.'

'He is a son of York, and he shall die!' cried Clifford, at the same time plunging his sword into the youth, who fell dead at his feet.

> '*Rutland.* O, let me pray before I take my death!
> To thee I pray, sweet Clifford, pity me!
> *Clifford.* Such pity as my rapier's point affords.
> *Rutland.* I never did thee harm; why wilt thou slay me?
> *Clifford.* Thy father did.
> *Rutland.* But 'twas ere I was born.
> Thou hast one son; for his sake pity me,
> Lest in revenge thereof—sith God is just—
> He be as miserably slain as I.
> Ah, let me live in prison all my days;
> And when I give occasion of offence,
> Then let me die, for now thou hast no cause.
> *Clifford.* No cause!
> Thy father slew my father; therefore, die.'
>
> *Henry VI., Part III.*, Act. i., s. 3.

For the credit of humanity it is a great relief to add the remarks of Clements Markham, who has investigated the evidence, upon this story. He says: 'The most absurd legend relating to the Battle of Wakefield is that told by Hall and Holinshed, and adopted by Shakespeare and nearly all modern historians, respecting the death of the Earl of Rutland. Hall says the young earl was scarcely of the age of twelve years; and, on this false foundation, he builds up the ridiculous legend. The fable rests on there being a child. If there was no child, nothing of the sort can have happened. Contemporary evidence is simply that, in retreating after the battle, Lord Clifford killed the Earl of Rutland on or near Wakefield Bridge. Edmund (the earl) was in his eighteenth year, and certainly sold his life dearly on the bridge. Hall's fable is a slander on Clifford and on the ill-fated young prince' (*Yorkshire Archæological Society's Journal*, part xxxiii.).

THE BATTLE OF TOWTON.

Towton, the saddest and the most destructive of the battles between the Houses of York and Lancaster, was fought on Palm Sunday, March 29th, 1461 A.D. The field lay on the side of the little river Cock, a tributary of the Wharfe, and some two or three miles from Tadcaster. Here met 100,000 Englishmen— 60,000 Red Rose and 40,000 White—and of these 36,000 are said to have been left dead on the field. The contest began (says tradition) in a blinding snowstorm; no quarter was given; the newly fallen snow became crimson with blood; and intimation of the terrible nature of the slaughter, taking place two or three miles away, was given to the inhabitants on the banks of the Wharfe, as they returned from their churches that morning, by the waters of that river being tinged with the crimson flood brought into it by the more deeply dyed stream of the Cock.

The writer does not know the author of the following lines, but they so beautifully embody these facts and traditions that he ventures to quote them:

'Where the red rose and the white rose
   In furious battle reel'd ;
And yeomen fought like barons,
   And barons died ere yield.

'Where mingling with the snow-storm
   The storm of arrows flew,
And York against proud Lancaster
   His ranks of spearmen threw.

'Where thunder-like the uproar
   Outshook from either side,
As hand to hand they battled
   From morn till eventide.

'Where the river ran all gory,
   And in hillocks lay the dead,
And seven and thirty thousand
   Fell from the white and red.'

Another story, related in the neighbourhood, is that the inhabitants of Towton had gone to their parish church at Saxton, and that while they were there the battle began and prevented them returning, so that they had to remain in the church the whole of the day:

'At Saxton Church the rustic peasants met;
When they returned the willows all were wet
With noble blood—astonished there they stand—
Thousands lie bleeding there on either hand.'

A well-known tradition relates to the death of Lord Dacres, of Gilsland, whose tomb is yet to be seen in Saxton Church. When Glover visited the place in 1585 (*i.e.*, 124 years after the battle), the account was thus related to him: 'Lord Dacres was slaine by a boy at Towton Field, which boy shot him out of a burtree-bush, when he had unclasped his helmet to drink a cup of wine, in revenge of his father, whom the said lord had slaine before, which tree hath been remarkable ever since by the inhabitants, and decayed within this few years. The place where he was slaine is called the North Acres, whereupon they have this rhyme:

> 'The Lord of Dacres
> Was slain in the North Acres.'

The place so named, the North Acres, is still, it is said, pointed out, and still burtree (or elder) bushes grow near it.

It is said that on a part of the field most remote from Saxton Richard III. began to erect a chapel, in order that prayer for the slain might there be made; but the completion was prevented by his death. At a very small distance from the battle-field, and on the banks of the Cock, stands the small and ancient chapel of Lede, or Lead, which may be the one alluded to. It was formerly extra-parochial, but now is annexed to the parish of Ryther.

The most beautiful of the legends connected with the Battle of Towton is that with regard to the rose, commonly known as the 'York and Lancaster rose.'

This rose, whose petals are variegated with mingled white and red, is said to have sprung up where the blood of York and Lancaster was so plentifully mingled. The bush (so it is said) refuses to grow elsewhere. If transplanted to other soil, it either fades away or the flowers revert to a single colour—white or red.

'There is a patch of wild white roses,
    That bloom on a battle-field,
Where the rival rose of Lancaster,
    Blushed redder still to yield;
Four hundred years have o'er them shed
    Their sunshine and their snow,
But, in spite of plough and harrow,
    Every summer there they blow.
Though rudely up to root them,
    With hand profane you toil,
The faithful flowers still fondly cluster,
    Around the sacred soil;
Though tenderly transplanted
    To the neatest garden gay,
Nor cost nor toil can tempt them
    There to live a single day.

'I ponder o'er their blossoms,
    And anon my busy brain
With bannered hosts and steel-clad knights
    Re-peopled all the plain—
I seemed to hear the lusty cheer
    Of the bowmen bold of York,
As they marked how well their cloth-yard shafts
    Had done their bloody work;
And steeds with empty saddles
    Came rushing wildly by,
And wounded warriors stagger'd past,
    Or only turned to die;
And the little sparkling river
    Was encumbered as of yore,
With ghastly corse of man and horse,
    And ran down red with gore.

'I started as I pondered,
    For loudly on my ear
Rose indeed a shout like thunder,
    A true good English cheer;

And the sound of drum and trumpet
  Came rolling up the vale,
And blazoned banners proudly flung
  Their glories to the gale ;
But not, oh ! not to battle did
  Those banners beckon now—
A baron stood beneath them,
  But not with helmèd brow,
And Yorkshire yeomen round him thronged,
  But not with bow and lance,
And the trumpet only bade them
  To the banquet and the dance.

'Again my brain was busy ;
  From out those flow'rets fair
A breath arose like incense—
  A voice of praise and prayer !
A silver voice that said, "Rejoice !
  And bless the God above,
Who has given thee these days to see,
  Of peace, and joy, and love.
Oh, never more by English hands
  May English blood be shed ;
Oh, never more be strife between
  The roses white and red !
The blessed words the shepherds heard,
  May we remember still—
" Throughout the world be peace on earth,
  And towards man, goodwill." '—*J. R. Planché*.

The legend has called forth many other poetical versions. The following pretty one appeared, with the signature of 'R——,' in *Blackwood's Magazine* many years ago :

THE ROSES OF TOWTON MOOR.

'Oh, the red and the white rose,
  As all the kingdom knows,

Were emblems of the foes
    In a sad and bloody work,
When old England's noblest blood
Was poured out in a flood,
To quench the burning feud
    Of Lancaster and York.

'For then the rival roses,
Worn by the rival houses,
The poor distracted nation
    Into rage and frenzy drove;
Tore the children from the mother,
Tore the sister from the brother,
And the broken-hearted lover
    From the lady of his love.

'When the Percys, Veres, and Nevilles
Left their castles, halls, and revels,
To rush like raging devils
    Into the deadly fight;
And loyalty and reason,
Confounded by the treason
That cast into a prison
    The King of yester night.

'Oh, the red and the white rose,
Upon Towton Moor it grows,
And red and white it blows
    Upon the swarth for evermore;
In memorial of the slaughter,
When the red blood ran like water,
And the victors gave no quarter,
    In the fight on Towton Moor;

'When the banners gay were beaming,
And the steel cuirasses gleaming,
And the martial music streaming,
    O'er that wide and lonely heath;

And many a heart was beating,
That dreamed not of retreating,
Which, ere the sun was setting,
    Lay still and cold in death;

'When the snow that fell at morning
Lay as a type and warning,
And stained and streaked with crimson,
    Like the roses white and red;
And filled each thirsty furrow,
With its token of the sorrow,
That wailed for many a morrow,
    Through the mansions of the dead.

'And now for twice two hundred years,
When the month of March appears,
All unchecked by plough or shears
    Spring the roses red and white;
Nor can the hand of mortal
Close the subterranean portal
That gives to life immortal
    These emblems of the fight.

'And as if they were enchanted,
Not a flower may be transplanted,
From these fatal precincts haunted
    By the spirits of the slain;
For howe'er the root you cherish,
It shall fade away and perish,
When removèd from the marish
    Of Towton's gory plain.

'But old Britannia now
Wears a rose upon her brow,
That blushing still doth glow,
    Like the Queen of all her race—
The rose that blooms victorious,
And, ever bright and glorious,
Shall continue to reign over us
    In mercy, love, and grace.'

Marston Moor Fight.

'Wouldst hear the tale? On Marston Heath
Met, front to front, the ranks of death;
Flourished the trumpets fierce, and how
Fired was each eye, and flush'd each brow;
On either side loud clamours ring,
"God save the cause!" "God save the King!"'

Scott.

The details of this battle, which sealed the fate of the Royal cause in the civil war of the seventeenth century, are matters of history. Legend and tradition have, however, several stories to relate.

The well in one of the cottage-gardens, in the village of Long Marston, is yet known as 'Cromwell's Well.' Here his Roundhead followers quenched their thirst before the battle, on the hot July day, and hence the village maidens bore the cooling draughts, in their milking-pails, to those who remained in martial array on the neighbouring hill-top.

The lane, still called Moor Lane, leading from the village to the moor, was the scene of one of the sharpest struggles in the battle; and here the belated villager meets phantom horsemen, headless or blood-covered, galloping to and fro, as if in the hurry and heat of battle.

At the western end of the village, says Mr. William Grainge, the indefatigable Yorkshire topographer, is Cromwell's Gap, an opening through three fences. Here no tree will grow. Quicksets have been repeatedly planted to fill up this gap, but they have always withered away, leaving the spaces exactly as they were before. Tradition's reason is, that here

Cromwell's soldiers cut down a number of the flying Royalists, and since then no tree or shrub will grow on the blood-stained soil. Another version is, that the hedges were cut down to make way for the cannon of the Parliamentary army, in order that they might be dragged into position on the rising-ground beyond. The ground once so dishonoured refuses, henceforth, to support the trees required to take the place of those removed for so base a purpose. 'The curse,' again to quote Grainge, 'or whatever it may be called, only extends to the wood of the hedges, and does not include the grass and the nettles, for they grow profusely in the gaps.'

Another story is that a shot from one of Cromwell's cannon entered the oven of a farmer named Gill in the village, as the family bread was baking, and, of course, wrought havoc therewith.

CROMWELL AND SIR R. GRAHAM.

Sir Richard Graham, of Norton Conyers, distinguished himself in the battle by acts of great bravery. When the day was irretrievably lost, and nothing was left but for every man to provide for his own security as best he could, Sir Richard, bleeding from twenty-six separate wounds, rode away, hoping to gain his home at Norton Conyers. This he did in the evening, but being completely exhausted, he was at once carried to his chamber, where within an hour he died. Cromwell, for some reason, is said to have had an inveterate hatred to this gentleman, and when he found that he had escaped from the field, he pursued him in person with a troop of horse. When he arrived at Norton Conyers he was informed that Graham was dead, and that the widow was weeping over the mangled corpse in the chamber of death. Possibly not satisfied with this answer, he burst into the chamber—it is said that he even rode his horse up the wide open staircase, and that the marks of its hoofs are still visible there, and on the landing—and found his enemy dead, as he had been told. It might have been thought that this was enough, but turning to the troopers who had followed him, he gave them permission to sack and despoil the house. This they did so effectually that everything which could not be carried off was destroyed.

CROMWELL AT RIPLEY.

The same evening, tradition relates, Cromwell, returning from pursuing a party of the Royalists (Sir R. Graham and his attendants, if the above story be true), arrived at Ripley, and proposed to stay for the night at the castle there, the house of the stanch Royalist, Sir William Ingleby. He sent one of his officers, a relative of the family, to announce his intention. The officer was told, by the porter of the gate, that Sir William was from home, but that his lady was within, and would receive any message he might wish to be conveyed to her. The officer sent in his name, and, obtaining an interview, informed the lady of the castle of his master's proposal. She at first replied: 'No such traitor shall enter here!' After some persuasion, and representation of the folly of resistance, she took her kinsman's advice, and consented to allow the general to remain for the night.

She received him at the gate of the lodge with a brace of pistols stuck in her apron-strings, and told him that she expected that both he and his soldiers would behave themselves properly while under her roof. She then led the way to the hall, and, pointing him to a sofa on which he sat down, she took her place on another directly opposite to him; and thus the two, equally jealous of each other's intentions, passed the night.

At his departure, in the morning, she observed 'that it was well for him that he had behaved so peaceably; for that, had it been otherwise, he would not have left the house alive.'

ANOTHER STORY.

Mary, daughter of Sir Francis Trappes, married Charles Townley, of Townley, in Lancashire, Esq., who was killed at the Battle of Marston Moor. During the engagement she was with her father near Knaresborough, where she heard of her husband's fate, and came upon the field, the next morning, to search for his body, while the attendants of the camp were stripping and burying the dead. Here she was accosted by a general officer, to whom she told her melancholy story. He heard her with great tenderness, but earnestly desired her to leave the place, where, beside the distress of witnessing such a scene, she might probably be insulted. She complied, and he called a trooper, who took her *en croupe*. On her way to Knaresborough, she inquired of the man the name of the officer to whose civility she had been indebted, and learned that it was Lieutenant-General Cromwell!

CAPTAIN LISTER: BATTLE OF TADCASTER, 1642.

At this battle, December 7th, 1642, between the Royalist forces of the Duke of Newcastle and the Parliamentarians under Lord Fairfax and his son, fell Captain Lister, a member of the Craven family of that name, and was interred in the churchyard at Tadcaster.

Thoresby, in his 'Ducatus Leodiensis,' relates the tradition that the son of Captain Lister, some years after the battle, was passing through the town, and, seeing the sexton digging a grave in the churchyard, he asked if he could tell him where the captain was buried. The man took up a skull, which he had just thrown out of the grave, and declared it was the skull of Captain Lister. On examination, a bullet-hole was found in it.

This incident so affected young Lister that he became ill and died a few hours afterwards.

'PITY POOR BRADFORD.' A LEGEND OF THE CIVIL WAR TIMES.

The Earl of Newcastle, commandant of the Royal forces, was besieging Bradford, in which he had shut up a portion of the Parliamentary army under Sir Thomas Fairfax. The old writer of 'A Genuine Account of the sore Calamities that befell Bradford in the time of the Civil War,' himself an eye-witness of the state of things in the town, says:

'In [the meantime the enemy (the Duke of Newcastle and his Royalists) took the opportunity of a parley to remove their cannon, and brought them nearer the town, and fixed them in a certain place called Goodman's End, directly against the heart of the town, and surrounding us on every side with horse and foot, so it was almost impossible for a single person to escape. Nor could the troops within the town act on the defensive for want of ammunition, which they had lost in their last defeat at Adwalton; nor had they a single match but such as were made of twisted cords dipped in oil. Oh! that dreadful and never-to-be-forgotten night, which was mostly spent in firing those deadly engines upon us; so that the blaze issuing therefrom appeared like lightning from heaven, the elements being, as it were, on fire, and the loud roaring of the cannon resembling the mighty thunders of the sky! This same night Sir Thomas Fairfax and the forces in his command cut their way through the besiegers and escaped from the town, thus leaving it more utterly at the Royalists' mercy.

'Now, reader, here stop—stop for a moment—pause, and suppose thyself in the like dilemma. Words cannot express, thoughts cannot imagine—nay, art itself is not able to paint out the calamities and woeful distresses with which we are now overwhelmed withal! Every countenance overspread with sorrow; every house overwhelmed with grief; husbands lamenting over their families; women wringing their hands in despair; children shrieking, crying, and clinging to their parents; Death, in all his dreadful forms and frightful aspects, stalking in every street and every corner! In short, horror, despair, and destruction united their efforts to spread devastation and complete our ruin!

'What are all our former calamities in comparison to these? Before there were some glimmering hopes of mercy from the enemy, but now they are fled—fled in every appearance. Our foes were exasperated with the opposition they had met with from us, but especially the cruel death by which the Earl of Newport's son fell by our unwary townsmen. For, behold! immediately orders were issued out to the soldiers by the Earl of Newcastle, their commander, that the next morning they should put to the sword every man, woman, and child, without regard to age, sex, or distinction whatsoever.'

The night before this sentence was to be carried out, the Earl of Newcastle was sleeping at Bolling, or Bowling, Hall. In the midst of the night a lady, clad in white gauzy garments from head to foot, entered the duke's bedroom, several times pulled the clothes from his bed, and then, when he was thoroughly aroused and trembling with fear, cried out with a lamentable voice, 'Pity poor Bradford! pity poor Bradford!' and then noiselessly departed.

'How far,' writes the narrator, 'this was true I submit it to others to determine. But this much I must affirm, that the hand of Providence never more conspicuously appeared in our favour, for, lo! immediately the earl countermanded the former order, and forbade the death of any person whatsoever, except only such as made resistance. Thus from a state of anguish and despair, we, who were but just ready to be swallowed up, by the wonderful providence of the Almighty, were reprieved as criminals from the rack. See what a surprising change immediately takes place:

the countenances of those, who were but just before overspread with horror and despair, begin in some measure to resume their former gaiety and cheerfulness—a general joy and gladness diffused itself through every breast; the hearts of those, who were ere now overwhelmed with sorrow, are now big with praise and thanksgiving to God for the wonderful and surprising deliverance brought about in their favour.'

VIII.

LEGENDS OF WELLS, LAKES, ETC.

SPRINGS and wells of water have, in all lands and in all ages, been greatly valued, and in some regarded with a feeling of veneration little, if at all, short of worship. They have yielded their treasure to the sustenance and refreshment of man and beast, as age after age of the world's history has passed along, and have been centres around which village story and gossip have gathered for generation after generation. Little wonder, therefore, is it that legends and traditions abound concerning them. These are often extremely local, and therefore little known. The names alone, however, suggest much. The memory of the mythical gods, satyrs, and nymphs of the ancient heathen times lingers in a few, as in Thors-kil or Thors-well, in the parish of Burnsall; and in the almost universal declaration—by which not over-wise parents seek to deter children from playing in dangerous proximity to a well—that at the bottom, under the water, dwells a mysterious being, usually named Jenny Green-teeth or Peg-o'-the-Well, who will certainly drag into the water any child who approaches too near to it.

The tokens of mediæval reverence for wells are abundant. The names of the saints to whom the wells were dedicated yet cling to them. 'There is scarcely a well of consequence in the United Kingdom,' says the editor of ' Lancashire Folk-lore,' ' which has not been solemnly dedicated to some saint in the Roman calendar.' Thus in Yorkshire we have Our Lady's Well or Lady Well, St. Helen's Well (very numerous), St. Margaret's Well at Burnsall, St. Bridget's Well near Ripon, St. Mungo's Well at Copgrove, St. John's Well at Beverley, St. Alkelda's Well at Middleham, etc. Dr. Whitaker remarks that the wells of Craven, which bear the names of saints, are invariably presided over by females, as was the case with wells under the pagan ritual, in which nymphs exclusively enjoyed the same honour.

Remnants of well-worship existed in Craven about the middle of the last century, when it was the custom on Sunday evenings for the young people to assemble and drink the waters mingled with sugar. This custom was particularly observed at St. Helen's Well at Eshton, and at Rouland Well, betwixt Rilstone and Hetton. 'These harmless and pleasing observances,' says the doctor, 'are now lost, and nothing better has been introduced into their place. It is, perhaps, as innocent at such hours of relaxation to drink water, even from a consecrated spring, as to swallow the poison of British distilleries at a public-house.'

Other wells there are whose designations preserve the names of owners, or historical personages, in olden times, as Ketel's (a Saxon nobleman) Well (Kettlewell), and the many Robin Hood's Wells; while the names of many others, as Beggar's-gill Well in Grasswood, near Kettlewell, the Drumming Well at Harpham, the Tailor's Well at Beverley, etc., preserve some topographical peculiarity or story, of more or less interest in local history, tradition, or folk-lore.

THE EBBING AND FLOWING WELL AT GIGGLESWICK.

About a mile from Settle, on the road leading towards Clapham, and at the foot of the high limestone cliff known as Giggleswick Scar, is the famous ebbing and flowing well. The water in this well periodically ebbs and flows, at longer or shorter intervals, according to the quantity running at the time. Sometimes the phenomenon takes place several times in the course of an hour, the water rising and sinking over a depth of several inches, and sometimes only once in the course of several hours. At one time it was thought there was some subterranean connection between the waters of this well and those of the ocean, and that the ebbing and flowing of the tides led to the rise and fall of the waters of the well. This is an improbable and unsatisfactory explanation. The true one is probably to be found in a system of natural syphons in the limestone rock. The theory that such is the case has been well worked out by a gentleman of the locality, whose name the writer is sorry he does not remember. Legend, however, has its own explanation, and this was admirably given by quaint Michael Drayton in his 'Polyolbion,' nearly 300 years ago (1573-1631).

'In all my spacious tract, let them, so wise, survey
My Ribble's rising banks, their worst, and let them say,

At Giggleswick, where I a fountain can you show,
That eight times in a day is said to ebb and flow.
Who sometime was a nymph, and in the mountains high
Of Craven, whose blue heads for caps put on the sky,
Amongst th' Oreads there, and Sylvans made abode
(It was ere human foot upon those hills had trod),
Of all the mountain kind, and, since she was most fair,
It was a Satyr's chance to see her silver hair
Flow loosely at her back, as up a cliffe she clame,
Her beauties noting well, her features, and her frame.
And after her he goes; which when she did espy,
Before him like the wind the nimble nymph doth fly;
They hurry down the rocks, o'er hill and dale they drive;
To take her he doth strain, t'outstrip him she doth strive,
As one his kind that knew, and greatly feared his rape,
And to the topick gods by praying to escape,
They turned her to a spring, which as she then did pant,
When wearied with her course her breath grew wondrous scant.
Even as the fearful nymph, then thick and short did blow,
Now made by them a spring, so doth she ebb and flow.'

LADY WELLS.

'Our Lady Wells,' that is, wells dedicated to the Virgin, are numerous in the country. One at Threshfield, near Linton, in Craven, has the attribute of being a place of safe refuge from all supernatural visitants—hobgoblins and the like.

Dr. Dixon ('Stories of Craven Dales') relates the story of a native, on his way home late at night from the public-house, being a spectator of some performances of Pam, the Threshfield Ghost, and his imps. Unfortunately the secret spectator sneezed, and then, in homely phrase, 'he had to run for it,' and only escaped condign punishment at the hands of the sprites by taking refuge in the very middle of 'Our

Lady's Well,' which they durst not approach. They, however, waited at such a distance as was permitted them, and kept their victim, nearly up to his neck in the cold water, until the crowing of the cock announced that the hour for their departure had arrived, when they fled, but not without vowing how severely they would punish him, if he ever again was caught eavesdropping at their parties.

At Thirsk, again, is a Lady Well. An old historian of the town says, ' In the marsh near the church flows a spring of pure and excellent water, commonly called Lady Well, doubtless a name of no modern description.' He also gives the following doggerel lines:

> ' Inspired by Greece's hallowed spring,
> Blandusia's fount let Horace sing;
> Whilst, favour'd by no music, I tell
> How much I love sweet Lady Well.
>
> ' Amidst the willow shades obscure,
> From age to age her stream runs pure;
> Yet has no seer aris'n to tell
> The bliss that flows from Lady Well.
>
> ' Save that in those dark distant days,
> When superstition dimm'd truth's rays,
> The monk promulgèd from his cell
> That virtue dwelt in Lady Well.'

ST. HELEN'S WELL.

There are more St. Helens than one, but the one to whom the many Yorkshire wells are supposed to be dedicated was Helen, or Helena, the mother of Constantine the Great, who was by birth a Yorkshire lady, or rather a British lady, from the neighbourhood of Eboracum. The waters of many of the wells bearing her name seem to have been deemed a specific for sore and weak eyes. This was the case with the one near Gargrave. Whitaker states that in his time votive offerings, such as ribbons and other decorative articles, were commonly to be seen tied to the bushes near these wells.

ST. JOHN'S WELL AT HARPHAM.

At Harpham, in the East Riding of Yorkshire, there is a well dedicated to St. John of Beverley, who is said to have been born in this village, and to have wrought many miracles through the virtue of the waters of this well. It is still believed to possess the power of subduing the wildest and fiercest animals. William of Malmesbury relates that in his time the most rabid bull, when brought to its waters, became quiet as the gentlest lamb.

THE DRUMMING WELL AT HARPHAM.

At the same village there is, in a field near the church, another well called the Drumming Well, to which appertains the following story, for which the writer is indebted to the *Leeds Mercury*.

About the time of the second or third Edward,—when all the young men of the country were required to be practised in the use of the bow, and for that purpose public 'butts' were found connected with almost every village, and occasionally 'field-days' for the display of archery were held, attended by gentry and peasant alike—the old manor house near this well at Harpham was the residence of the family of St. Quintin. In the village lived a widow, reputed to be somewhat 'uncanny,' named Molly Hewson. She had an only son, Tom Hewson, who had been taken into the family at the manor; and the squire, struck with his soldierly qualities, had appointed him trainer and drummer to the village band of archers.

A grand field-day of these took place in the well-field, in front of the manor house. A large company was assembled, and the sports were at their height, the squire and his lady looking on with the rest. But one young rustic proving more than usually stupid in the use of his bow, the squire made a rush forward to chastise him. Tom, the drummer, happened to be standing in his way, and near the well. St. Quintin accidentally ran against him and sent him staggering backward, and tripping, he fell head foremost down the well. Some time elapsed before he could be extricated, and when this was effected the youth was dead. The news spread quickly, and soon his mother appeared upon the scene. At first she was frantic, casting herself upon his body, and could not realize—though she had been warned of the danger of this spot to her son—that he was dead. Suddenly she rose up and stood, with upright mien, outstretched arm, and stern composure, before the squire. She remained silent awhile, glaring upon him with dilated eyes, while the awe-stricken bystanders gazed upon her as if she were some supernatural being. At length she broke the silence, and, in a sepulchral tone of voice, exclaimed—'Squire St. Quintin, you were the friend of my boy, and would still have been his friend but for this calamitous mishap.

You intended not his death, but from your hand his death has come. Know, then, that through all future ages, whenever a St. Quintin, Lord of Harpham, is about to pass from life, my poor boy shall beat his drum at the bottom of this fatal well; it is I—the wise woman, the seer of the future—that say it.'

The body was removed and buried; and from that time, so long as the old race of St. Quintin lasted, on the evening preceding the death of the head of the house, the rat-tat of Tom's drum was heard in the well by those who listened for it.

WORDSWORTH'S HART-LEAP WELL.

This well, situated near the road leading from Richmond in Swaledale to Askrigg in Wensleydale, has been immortalized by Wordsworth's version of the legend, according to which it receives its name.

In the early morning of a long summer's day, in the far-off mediæval times, a blithe company of ladies, lords, knights, and esquires of Wensleydale assembled to hunt the deer. A noble hart soon led them merrily up the dale. For hour after hour they followed; but as the day began to wane, and still the chase continued, one after another fell away, until a solitary knight (Sir Walter) alone was left, with two or three of the dogs, on the trail of the hunted beast. The rest must be told in the poet's own words:

'The knight hallooed, he chid, and cheered them on,
  With suppliant gestures and upbraiding stern;
But breath and eyesight fail; and one by one
  The dogs are stretched among the mountain fern.

'Where is the throng, the tumult of the race?
  The bugles that so joyfully were blown?
This chase it looks not like an earthly chase;
  Sir Walter and the hart are left alone.

'The poor hart toils along the mountain-side;
  I will not stop to tell how far he fled,
Nor will I mention by what death he died;
  But now the knight beholds him lying dead.

'Dismounting then he leans against a thorn;
  He had no follower, dog, nor man, nor boy;
He neither smacked his whip nor blew his horn,
  But gazed upon the spoil with silent joy.

  .   .   .   .

'Upon his side the hart was lying stretched;
  His nose half-touched a spring beneath a hill;
And with the last deep groan his breath had fetched
  The waters of the spring were trembling still.

'And now, too happy for repose or rest
  (Was never man in such a joyful case!),
Sir Walter walked all round, north, south, and west,
  And gazed and gazed upon the darling place.

'And climbing up the hill—it was at least
  Nine roods of sheer ascent—Sir Walter found
Three several hoof-marks, which the hunted beast
  Had left imprinted on the verdant ground.

'Sir Walter wiped his face, and cried, "Till now
  Such sight was never seen by living eyes;
Three leaps have borne him from this lofty brow
  Down to the very fountain where he lies.

'"I'll build a pleasure-house upon this spot,
  And a small arbour make for rural joy;
'Twill be the traveller's shed, the pilgrim's cot,
  A place of love for damsels that are coy.

' " A cunning artist will I have to frame
    A basin for that fountain in the dell!
And they who do make mention of the same,
    From this day forth, shall call it Hart Leap Well.

' " And, gallant brute! to make thy praises known,
    Another monument shall here be raised;
Three several pillars, each a rough-hewn stone,
    And planted where thy hoofs the turf have grazed.

. . . .

' " Till the foundations of the mountains fail
    My mansion with its arbour shall endure,
The joy of them who till the fields of Swale,
    And them who dwell among the woods of Ure."

. . . .

' Ere thrice the moon into her port had steered,
    A cup of stone received the living well.
Three pillars of rude stone Sir Walter reared,
    And built a house of pleasure in the dell.

' And near the fountain, flowers of stature tall,
    With trailing plants and trees were intertwined,—
Which soon composed a little sylvan hall,
    A leafy shelter from the sun and wind.

' And thither when the summer days were long,
    Sir Walter journey'd with his paramour;
And with the dancers and the minstrel's song,
    Made merriment within that pleasant bower.

' The knight, Sir Walter, died in course of time,
    And his bones lie in his paternal vale,—
But there is matter for a second rhyme,
    And I to this would add another tale.'

The 'second rhyme,' containing the sequel to the story, is perhaps, as a poetical effort and version of the legend, more beautiful than the story itself, and as exhibiting Wordsworth's sensitiveness to the cruelties of the chase, and as recording local tradition and superstition, cannot, though somewhat lengthy, be omitted here.

The poet is supposed to visit the place when many years have passed away since

> 'The knight, Sir Walter, died in course of time.'

He thus recounts what he saw and heard:

> ' As I from Hawes to Richmond did repair,
>   It chanced that I saw, standing in a dell,
> Three aspens at three corners of a square;
>   And one, not four yards distance, near a well.
>
> ' What this imported I could ill divine;
>   And, pulling now my rein, the horse to stop,
> I saw three pillars standing in a line,
>   The last stone pillar on a dark hill-top.
>
> ' The trees were gray, with neither arms nor head;
>   Half-wasted the square mound of tawny green;
> So that you just might say, as then I said,
>   " Here in old time the hand of man hath been."
>
> ' I looked upon the hill both far and near,
>   More doleful place did never eye survey;
> It seemed as if the spring-time came not here,
>   And Nature here were willing to decay.
>
> ' I stood in various thoughts and fancies lost,
>   When one who was in shepherd's garb attired
> Came up the hollow: him did I accost,
>   And what this place might be I then inquired.
>
> ' The shepherd stopped, and that same story told
>   Which in my former rhyme I have rehearsed.
>   " A jolly place," said he, " in times of old;
>   But something ails it now; the spot is curst.

' " You see these lifeless stumps of aspen wood—
  Some say that they are beeches, other elms—
These were the bower; and here a mansion stood,
  The finest palace of a hundred realms!

' " The arbour does its own condition tell;
  You see the stones, the fountain, and the stream;
But as to the great lodge! you might as well
  Hunt half a day for a forgotten dream.

' " There's neither dog nor heifer, horse nor sheep,
  Will wet his lips within that cup of stone;
And oftentimes, when all are fast asleep,
  This water doth send forth a dolorous groan.

' " Some say that here a murder has been done,
  And blood cries out for blood; but for my part,
I've guessed, when I've been sitting in the sun,
  That it was all for that unhappy hart.

' " What thoughts must through the creature's brain have passed!
  Even from the topmost stone, upon the steep,
Are but three bounds—and look, sir, at this last,
  O master! it has been a cruel leap.

' " For thirteen hours he ran a desperate race,
  And in my simple mind we cannot tell
What cause the hart might have to love this place,
  And come and make his death-bed near the well.

' " Here on the grass perhaps asleep he sank,
  Lulled by this fountain in the summer-tide;
This water was, perhaps, the first he drank,
  When he had wandered from his mother's side.

' " In April, here beneath the scented thorn,
  He heard the birds their morning carols sing;
And he, perhaps, for aught we know, was born
  Not half a furlong from that self-same spring.

> ' " But now here's neither grass nor pleasant shade,
>   The sun on drearier hollow never shone;
> So will it be, as I have often said,
>   Till trees, and stones, and fountain all are gone."
>
> ' " Gray-headed shepherd, thou hast spoken well;
>   Small difference lies between thy creed and mine;
> This beast not unobserved by Nature fell;
>   His death was mourned by sympathy divine.
>
> . . . .
>
> ' " One lesson, shepherd, let us two divide,
>   Taught both by what she shows and what conceals,
> Never to blend our pleasure or our pride,
>   With sorrow of the meanest thing that feels." '

THE LEGEND OF SEMERWATER.

The legend of a town suddenly engulfed by water, and the site of it henceforth becoming a lake, is common in both the Old and the New World. Its remote origin is probably to be found in the Scripture narrative of the destruction of the cities of the plain, and the formation thereby of the Dead Sea.

Of two Yorkshire lakes at least the story is told—viz., Semerwater, or Simmerwater, in Wensleydale, and Gormire, near Thirsk.

A few miles above the well-known Aysgarth Force, on the river Ure, there enters that river, on its southern bank, a tributary called the Bain. Ascending this river for two or three miles, the lake Semerwater is reached. It occupies a wild, solitary spot among the mountains,—Addleborough, 1,565 feet above the sea-level, and The Stake, 1,840 feet, towering above it. It is about three miles in circumference. Opening out at its upper end, between the mountains, are three deep, rugged ravines—Raydale, Bardale, and Cragdale—down each of which pours a mountain torrent. On a calm summer's day, the lake is an embodiment of the ideas of peace and repose, in retirement from the world; but when the floods descend from the surrounding moors and mountains, and the western winds rush down the ravines at its head, its waters rise many feet in an incredibly short time, and it becomes truly 'a troubled sea,' and vast volumes of its waters, being driven over its eastern bank, flood the lowlands of the valley beneath.

The legend as to its formation is thus told:

In the spot, which it now occupies, there once stood a town of considerable size. Under the guise of a poor beggar-man, ragged, hungry, and old, there came an angel to the town. He begged from door to door until he had visited every house, but found commiseration and relief at none. As he left it, just outside the town, he came upon a humble cottage inhabited by an aged and poverty-stricken couple. To them he repeated his tale of want. Immediately they asked him to enter their humble dwelling, and they brought forth for him the best they had—bread and milk and cheese. After he had appeased his hunger he thanked and blessed them, and at their solicitation passed the night under their roof. At his departure in the morning he stood by his friends' abode, and, looking back over the hard-hearted, uncharitable town, lifted up his hands and repeated the following lines:

> 'Semerwater rise! Semerwater sink!
> And swallow the town, all save this house,
> Where they gave me meat and drink.'

No sooner said than done. The waters of the valley rose; the town sunk and disappeared beneath them. But as they approached the hospitable cottage, 'there their proud waves were stayed;' and even yet a small old house near the lower end of the lake is pointed out as all that is left of the once flourishing town. To some eyes—those of persons gifted with second, or double sight, it is presumed—the roofs and chimneys of the other houses at the bottom are visible through the waters. Perhaps some reader, who visits the place, may be able thus to detect them.

This legend, as several other of our Yorkshire legends, has been, with a little variation in detail, beautifully embalmed in our county's poetry by Susan K. Phillips in the following verses :

'At the base of mighty Addlebro' fair glimmers Seamer Water,
Where the dales send many a stalwart son, and many a soft-eyed daughter,
To linger 'neath the larches, and watch the bright becks leap,
From Raydale and from Bardale, to their home in Seamer deep.

. . . .

'Deep in the heart of Wensleydale fair Seamer Water lies,
Where the lark springs up to carol in the pale blue northern skies ;
Where the trout and bream are leaping, where the silvery willows quiver,
Where long-haired birches wave their locks when June's soft breezes shiver.

' And yet eight hundred years ago, ere ever Conan gave
The meadow lands where Byland monks built Jervaulx's stately nave,
The traveller scaling Addlebro' gazed from the summit there
On towers, and streets, and guarded walls, that girt a city fair.

'One summer eve the sinking sun shone full on Whitefell Foss,
As an aged man strove wearily the brawling stream to cross,
As through romantic Cragdale he tottered feebly on,
And sought for rest and welcome from hearts that gave him none.

'At priestly door, at serf's low hut, at baron's lordly hall,
He prayed for food and shelter, and prayed in vain to all,
Till old, and worn, and lonely, the cruel streets he left,
And crawled into a lowly cot, hid in the mountain's cleft.

'"For the sake of Christ, I pray you for charity," he said,
The peasant brought his cup of milk, he brought his crust of bread,
And shared his scanty pittance with the wanderer who came
To ask for human mercy in the God of mercy's name.

'The old man ate and drank, and lo, his form and aspect seemed
To change before the peasant's eyes as unto one who dreamed;
Right royally he trod the floor, right royally he spoke—
"My blessing on the homestead where the bread of life I broke."

'Out on the steep hillside he strode, he raised his staff on high,
He shook it where the sleeping town lay 'neath the evening sky.
"I call thee, Seamer Water, rise fast, rise deep, rise free,
'Whelm all except the little house that fed and sheltered me!"

'And fast rose Seamer Water in answer to his word,
From beck, and foss, and tribute-stream, the floods obedient poured,
And all the air seemed booming with a mighty funeral knell,
'Mid shriek, and shout, and frantic prayer, to earth the peasant fell.

'And when at sunrise painfully he roused him from his swoon,
His cot stood safe, and from his side his awful guest had gone,

But where at eve the city proud stood busy, strong, and gay,
Fair Seamer Water glittered to hail the wakening day.

'It is eight hundred years ago, and legends dim and fade,
But still men say at Hallowe'en, beneath the larches' shade,
Whoso in Seamer Water at sunset gazes down,
Sees town, and street, and battlement—the shadow of the town.'

GORMIRE.

The legend as to Gormire—a small lake romantically situated on the slope of the Hambleton Hills, at the foot of Whitestone Cliff, a few miles from the town of Thirsk—is in many respects similar to that of Seamerwater. Here once stood a populous town; but, in this case, the calamity which destroyed it was an earthquake. In a moment, by a convulsion of the earth, an abyss in the mountain-side was opened, and into it sank the whole population, with houses and all that belonged to them. Soon a body of water, *unfathomable* and *bottomless*, rolled over the spot; though, in spite of this marvellous condition of the lake, 'it is asserted that the tops of the houses, and the desolate chimneys, are sometimes visible to the astonished eyes of the visitor who embarks upon these mysterious waters.'

IX.

MISCELLANEOUS LEGENDS, ETC.

THE SWINE HARRIE; OR, 'HOIST ON HIS OWN PETARD.'

THERE is a legend, common to many parts of England and to other countries also, which describes how the theft of an animal was visited upon the thief by means of his victim. In some places the animal was a deer, in another a dog, and in America even a corpse.

In Yorkshire it was a pig or swine. On the side of Pinnow Hill, in Lothersdale, is a field called Swine Harrie. 'To harrie' means, in the language of these northern parts, to hunt with the object of theft or plunder; so that the name 'Swine Harrie' indicates a place at which such a theft of swine was committed. The legend connected with it is this:

In far-off days a man, having stolen a pig, was leading it home in the dead of night by a string. Crossing this field, he came to one of the high stone walls common in the neighbourhood, over which was a stile formed by two ladders, one placed on each side of the wall, and united at the top. Over this it was necessary to lift his prize. Therefore, taking the pig in his arms, and throwing the loose end of the string over his shoulder, he ascended the ladder; but when at the top the animal, plunging, slipped from his arms over the wall, and, losing his foothold on the steps, he also fell—the swine on the one side, and the thief on the other—and, the string having become entangled round his neck, both were suspended thereby. In the morning they were thus found—the man dead.

In Charnwood Forest there is the same legend, only there the animal was a deer; and the place at which the tragedy occurred is yet known as Deadman's Stone. The following are the chief parts of a poetical version of the story, quoted by the late Dr. Dixon in 'Tales of Craven Dales':

> 'John of Oxley had watched on the round Cat Hill,
>   He had "harried" all Timber Wood;
> Each rabbit and hare said "Ha! ha!" to his snare,
>   But the venison, he knew, was good.

> 'A herd was resting beneath the broad oak
>   (The ranger, he knew, was a-bed);
> One shaft he drew on his well-tried yew,
>   And a gallant hart lay dead.

> 'He tied its legs, and he hoisted his prize,
>   And he toiled over Lubcloud Brow;
> He reached the tall stone standing out alone—
>   Standing then as it standeth now.

> 'With his back to the stone, he rested his load,
>   And he chuckled with glee to think,
> That the rest of the way on the down-hill lay,
>   And his wife would have spiced the drink.

> 'The "rest of the way" John Oxley ne'er trod
>   That ale was untouched by him;

In the morning gray there were looks that way,
  But the mountain mists were dim.

'Days past—he came not—his children play'd—
  And wept—then gamboll'd again ;
They saw with surprise their mother's wet eyes
  Were still on the hills—in vain.

  .   .   .   .   .

'A swineherd was passing o'er Great Ives Head,
  When he noticed a motionless man ;
He shouted in vain—no reply could he gain—
  So he down to the gray stone ran.

'There was Oxley's corpse on one side the stone,
  On the other the down-hanging deer ;
The burden had slipp'd, and his neck it had nipped—
  He was hang'd by his prize—all was clear.

'The gallows still stands upon Shepeshed high lands
  As a mark for the poachers to own,
How the wicked will get within their own net,
  And 'tis called "The Gray Hangman's Stone."

UPSALL AND ITS CROCKS OF GOLD.

High up on a spur of the Hambleton Hills, overlooking the great Vale of York and the hills beyond it, and the whole country, from York into the county of Durham, stands the small village of Upsall. The old castle, of which scarcely a fragment remains, was in olden times a stronghold and favourite residence of the Scroopes. The modern 'castle,' the seat of Captain Turton, standing near the site of the old one, is one of the palatial houses of Yorkshire. The name is a Scandinavian one, and in many aspects an interesting and remarkable one. 'Even,' writes a learned Dane (Worsaal), 'the name of one of the most important sacrificial places in the Scandinavian north is to be found in Yorkshire, in Upsall (from Upsalier), the High Halls.'

Well, 'at the village of Upsall resided many years ago,' writes Mr. William Grainge in his admirable 'History of the Vale of Mowbray,' 'a man who dreamed, on three nights successively, that if he went to London Bridge he would hear of something greatly to his advantage. He went, travelling the whole distance from Upsall to London on foot. Having arrived there, he took up his station on the bridge, where he waited until his patience was nearly exhausted, and the idea that he had acted a very foolish part began to rise in his mind. At length he was accosted by a Quaker, who kindly inquired what he was waiting there so long for. After some hesitation he told his dreams. The Quaker laughed at his simplicity, and told him that he had had that night a very curious dream himself, which was, that if he went and dug under a certain bush in Upsall Castle Yard, in Yorkshire, he would find a pot of gold; but he did not know where Upsall was, and inquired of the countryman if he knew? Seeing some advantage in secrecy, he pleaded ignorance of the locality, and then, thinking his business in London was completed, returned immediately home, dug beneath the bush, and there found a pot filled with gold, and on the cover an inscription he did not understand. The pot and the cover were, however, preserved at the village inn, where one day a bearded stranger, like a Jew, made his appearance, saw the pot, and read the inscription, the plain English of which was:

" "Look lower—where this stood
Is another twice as good."

The man of Upsall, hearing this, resumed his spade, returned to the bush, dug deeper, and found another pot filled with gold, far more valuable than the first. On the second pot the inscription of the first was repeated. Encouraged by this, he dug deeper still, and found another yet more valuable.

'This story has been related of other places, but Upsall appears to have as good a claim to it as any other. Here we have the constant tradition of the inhabitants, and the identical bush yet remains beneath which the treasure was found—an old elder bush, near the north-west corner of the ruins.'

HAVERAH PARK.—A LAME LEGEND.

Some five or six miles to the west of Knaresborough, in the heart of what was once the Royal Forest, is a district, consisting of several farms, named Haverah Park, and which for two centuries has belonged to the Ingilbys of Ripley Castle.

This place was probably at one time an enclosed area, or 'park,' within the forest, for the better preservation of the deer and the convenience of hunting, and derived its name from *Haie*, a hedge or fence, and *wra*, or *roe*, a kind of deer; thus meaning—*Haie-wra*—the fenced place, or enclosure, for deer.

But legend and philology are often widely at variance And so in this case, for the former thus accounts for the name of the park:

There was, in the days when the great John o' Gaunt was lord of the Forest of Knaresborough, a certain man named Havera, a cripple, whose only means of progress was by the help of crutches. This man had the good fortune one day to meet with the great lord as he was hunting in the forest.

'My lord,' said the cripple, 'I crave of your bounty permission to enclose a small quantity of land, by tillage of which I may obtain sustenance.'

The prince acceded to the request, and made a grant in the following terms:

> 'I, John o' Gaunt,
> Do give and do grant,
> To thee, Havera,
> As much of my ground
> As thou canst hop round
> In a long summer's day.'

Havera gladly accepted these terms, saw that his crutches were in good order, and, selecting Barnaby Day (June 11th), one of the longest in the year, proceeded to his task. Commencing at sunrise, and hopping away without cessation until sunset, he so nearly completed the circuit of what is now the park that, just as the orb of day was disappearing below the western horizon, he was able to throw one of his crutches to the point whence he started, before the sun totally disappeared, and thus to surround, and win for himself, the district which has ever since borne his name—Haverah Park.

A WILD BOAR LEGEND.

There is another legend connected with Haverah Park.

Two patches of woodland, on the southern side of the valley (in the Park), bear the names of High and Low Boarholes, and to one of them the following legend attaches itself:

Once upon a time (unfortunately, the exact time is not given) a king of England was hunting in the forest, and, becoming separated from his retinue, was attacked in this dell by an old wild boar, which, having seized in its mouth the weapon of the royal hunter, snatched it from his hand, and, proceeding to follow up this advantage, was in a fair way to putting an end to the reign of an English sovereign, when, by chance, one of the attendant knights came on the scene, and, attacking the animal vigorously with his boar-spear, succeeded in killing it, and so delivered the life of his monarch from imminent danger. The name of this knight was Ingilby, and, as a token of royal gratitude to him and his descendants for ever, the King granted the park in which the occurrence took place.

To the family of Ingilby the lands certainly now belong; but their tenure of them, unfortunately for the legend, only dates from the time of Charles II., when wild boars had been long extinct.

'The whole story,' remarks Mr. William Grainge, 'is a myth—probably a stray shaft from the long-bow of some former forester.'

DE LACY AND LORD DACRE'S DAUGHTER.

The following legendary ballad relates to the same place, and is from the pen of the late Stephen Fawcett, a local poet of considerable power. De Lacy's knowledge of the place may have been due to some of the hunting expeditions in the Royal Park.

' " Where art thou going, sweet shepherdess,
    Where art thou going so early?"
" My flocks I feed in Haverah's Mead,
    When the dew is shining clearly."

' " Drops of dew, on starry blue,
    Never knew such beauty;
Haverah's maid I came not to wed,
    But love has conquered duty."

' " Ride on, ride on, De Lacy bold,
    I trust no traitorous lover;
My low degree were shame to thee—
    I fear thou art a rover!"

' " Lord Dacre's child I will not wed,
    By Heaven I've sworn already;
Of castle, town, and dale and down,
    Thou only shalt be lady."

' " Ride on, ride on," she archly cried,
    " For I soothly vow and fairly,
No shepherdess shalt thou caress,
    Shouldst love her e'er so dearly.

' " Lord Dacre is a gruesome carle,
    To ruth and fear a stranger;
But wizards say, ' Love bears no nay.'
    So be thine the shame and danger."

' He merrily placed her on his steed,
    Tripped like a page beside her,
With glancing stream, and dew-drop beam,
    Merrily glanced the rider.

He placed her on his palfrey proud,
    And sought a hermit's dwelling,
Where kneeling he in sanctity
    His rosary was telling.

'The hermit rose and wedded them,
   O'er holy missal bending,
Sweet strains of love from Haverah's Grove,
   On morning wing ascending.

'"Thou art beguiled," she cried, "De Lacy,"
   As in his arms he caught her;
"Thy oath and word are broke, false lord—
   I am Lord Dacre's daughter."

'De Lacy gazed, confused, amazed,
   Upon the lovely speaker;
And the captive now was led to bow
   Before the great Lord Dacre.'

The Beggar's or Lover's Bridge at Egton.

At Egton, near Whitby, the river Esk is spanned by a bridge known, in popular parlance, as the Beggar's Bridge, and also as the Lover's Bridge. The story of the origin of the former name is that a certain man, named Thomas Ferrers, a beggar, either born at Egton or coming into the neighbourhood in early life, was crossing the river, when swollen, at this place by means of the stepping-stones, which then afforded the only means of crossing, and, falling in, was nearly drowned. He then made a vow that, if he should ever have the means to do so, he would build a bridge at the spot for the convenience and safety of all future wayfarers. He journeyed to Hull, and in that town, in the course of time, rose to riches and eminence. Nor did he forget his vow. He built a good bridge of one large and elegant arch, on which are inscribed his initials and the date, 1621 A.D. Hence arose the name of the Beggar's Bridge. In Trinity

Church, Hull, there is a large monument to the memory of Alderman Thomas Ferrers and his wife, showing the date of the death of this benefactor to his county to have been in 1631 A.D.

The other name, Lover's Bridge, is explained in the following portion of a version of the legend by Mrs. George Dawson, and given in 'Ballads of Yorkshire,' edited by Ingledew. It bears, however, the heading

THE BEGGAR'S BRIDGE.

'The dalesmen say that their light archway
   Is due to an Egton man,
Whose love was tried by a 'whelming tide.
I heard the tale in its native vale,
   And thus the legend ran:

'"Why lingers my loved one? Oh, why does he roam
On the last winter evening that hails him at home?
He promised to see me once more ere he went,
But the long rays of gloaming all lonely I've spent.
The stones at the fording no longer I see;
Ah! the darkness of night has concealed them from me!"

'The maiden of Glaisdale sat lonely at eve,
And the cold, stormy night saw her hopelessly grieve;
But when she looked forth from her casement at morn,
The maiden of Glaisdale was truly forlorn!
For the stones were engulfed where she looked for them last,
By the deep swollen Esk, that rolled rapidly past;
And vainly she strove, with her tear-bedimmed eye,
The pathway she gazed on last night to descry.

'Her lover had come to the brink of the tide,
And to stem its swift current repeatedly tried;
But the rough whirling eddy still swept him ashore,
And relentlessly bade him attempt it no more.

Exhausted, he climbed the steep side of the brae,
And looked up the dale ere he turned him away;
Ah! from her far window a light flickered dim,
And he knew she was faithfully watching for him.

> ' " I go seek my fortune, love,
>   In a far, far distant land,
>   And without thy parting blessing, love,
>   I am forced to quit the strand.
>
> ' " But over Arncliff's brow, my love,
>   I see thy twinkling light;
>   And when deeper waters part us, love,
>   'Twill be my beacon bright.
>
> ' " If fortune ever favour me,
>   St. Hilda, hear my vow!
>   No lover again in my native plain
>   Shall be thwarted as I am now.
>
> ' " One day I'll come to claim my bride
>   As a worthy and wealthy man;
>   And my well-earned gold shall raise a bridge
>   Across this torrent's span."

' The rover came back from a far-distant land,
And he claimed of the maiden her long-promised hand;
But he built, ere he won her, the bridge of his vow,
And the lovers of Egton pass over it now.'

THE WHITE HORSE OF THE STRID, OR THE THREE SISTERS OF BEAMSLEY.

There is a tradition connected with the Strid, near Bolton Bridge, on the river Wharfe, that on the morning of the May-day preceding any fatal accident in that river, a spectral white horse, the steed of the queen of the fairies, is to be seen arising from the spray and mist around the foaming cataract. The following legend of three sisters, co-heiresses of

Beamsley Hall, each, while watching for the fairy steed, expressing the desire she would wish to realize by the magic of the fairy's wand, and after the appearance to them of the mystic white horse perishing in the waters, is founded upon this tradition. Beamsley, or, as it was anciently spelt, 'Bethmeslie,' is a hamlet and scattered township near Bolton Bridge. Its hall, at the foot of Howber Hill, often called Beamsley Beacon, was the home of the Mauleverer family from the time of the Conquest to the fourteenth century, when it passed by marriage to the Claphams.

Both these families are buried in the same vault in the Abbey Church at Bolton, and it is of them that Wordsworth writes:

> 'Pass, pass who will yon chantry door,
> And, through the chink in the fractured floor,
> Look down, and see a grisly sight;
> A vault where the bodies are buried upright!
> There, face to face, and hand to hand,
> The Claphams and Mauleverers stand;
> And in his place, among son and sire,
> Is John de Clapham, that fierce esquire—
> A valiant man, and a man of dread
> In the ruthless wars of the White and Red;
> Who dragged Earl Pembroke from Banbury Church,
> And smote off his head on the stones of the porch.'

To one or other of these two families it must be supposed that the three sisters of the legend belonged.

The beautiful verses embodying the legend 'originally appeared,' says Dr. Dixon, 'in *The European Magazine*, from whence they were transferred to the "Poetic Album" of Alaric Watts. They are said to be from the pen of a lady, a native of York, but who was long located in Craven.'

'"Oh, sisters, hasten we on our way—
  The Wharfe is wide and strong;
Our father alone in his hall will say,
  'My daughters linger long.'
Yet, tarry awhile in the yellow moonlight,
And each shall see her own true knight.

'" For now in her boat of an acorn-shell
  The fairy queen may be,
She dives in a water-spider's bell
  To keep her revelry;
We'll drop a thistle's beard in the tide—
'Twill serve for bridles when fairies ride;
And she who shall first her white horse see
Shall be the heiress of Bethmeslie."

'Then Jeanette spoke with her eyes of light:
  "Oh, if I had fairy power,
I would change this elm to a gallant knight,
  And this gray rock to a bower!
Our dwelling should be behind a screen
Of blossoming alders and laurustine;
Our hives should tempt the wild bees all,
  And the swallows love our eaves,
For the eglantine should tuft our wall,
  And cover their nests with leaves;
The spindle's wool should lie unspun,
And our lambs lie safe in the summer's sun,
While the merry bells ring for my knight and me,
Farewell to the halls of Bethmeslie."

'Then Annette shook her golden hair:
  "If I had power and will,
These rocks should change to marble rare,
  And the oaks should leave the hill,

To build a dome of prouder height
Than ever yet rose in the morning light,
And every one of these slender reeds
   Should be a page in green,
To lead and deck my berry-brown steeds
   And call my greyhounds in;
These lilies should all be ladies gay,
To weave the pearls for my silk array,
   And none but a princely knight should see
   Smiles in the lady of Bethmeslie."

'Then softly said their sister May:
   "I would ask neither spell nor wand,
For better I prize this white rose spray
   Plucked by my father's hand;
And little I heed the knight to see
Who seeks the heiress of Bethmeslie!
Yet would I give one of these roses white
   If the fairy queen would ride
Safe o'er this flood ere the dead of night,
   And bear us by her side;
And then with her wing let her lift the latch
Of my father's gate, and his slumbers watch.
And touch his eyes with her glow-worm gleam,
Till he sees and blesses us in his dream!"

'The night winds howled o'er Bolton Strid,
   The flood was dark and drear;
And thro' it swam the Fairy Queen's steed,
   The Lady May to bear;
And that milk-white steed was seen to skim
Like a flash of the moon on the water's brim.
The morning came, and the winds were tame,
   The flood slept on the shore;
But the sisters three of Bethmeslie
   Returned to its hall no more.

'Now under the shade of its ruined wall
　　A thorn grows lonely, bare and tall;
And there a weak and weeping weed
　　Seems on its rugged stem to feed;
The shepherds sit in the green recess,
And call them Pride and Idleness.
But there the root of a white rose-tree
　　Still blooms at the gate of Bethmeslie.

'Woe to the maid that on morn of May
　　Shall see that White Horse rise;
The hope of her heart shall pass away
　　As the foam of his nostrils flies,
Unless to her father's knees she brings,
The white rose-tree's first offerings.

There is no dew from summer skies
Has power like the drop from a father's eyes;
And if on her cheek that tear of bliss
Shall mingle with his holy kiss,
The bloom of her cheek shall blessed be
　　As the fairy rose of Bethmeslie.'

OSMOTHERLEY.

At a distance of seven miles from Northallerton, up in the Cleveland hillside, is a village named Osmotherley. The name, in all probability, is derived from an early owner named 'Osmund,' and 'ley,' a field or meadow; and thus means the field of Osmund. Legend, however, tells a different story.

Osmund, says the story, was King of Northumbria. He and his queen had an only child, named Oswy, the heir of his kingdom.

The augurs, or wise men, were consulted at the child's birth as to its future fortunes. They united in declaring that when the child arrived at a certain age—even naming the day—it would be drowned. The princess, its mother, was determined to prevent such a catastrophe, and as the time approached she fled with the boy to the top of Osnaberg, now better known as Roseberry Topping. Here—far away, as she thought, from any watery depths—she awaited the passing of the fatal day. But, overcome by heat and fatigue, she fell asleep, and the young prince wandered away from her side, until he came to a small spring of water, issuing from the mountain-side, and forming a small well.

A local poet, J. W. Ord, has beautifully told the sequel:

> 'Then weary of his dalliance,
>   He sought the grassy mound,
> Plucked oft the azure harebell,
>   The foxglove tapering round;
> And then, oh, lovely vision!
>   Beneath the mountain-brow,
> A fountain, clear, enchanting,
>   With heaven's own colours true.'

Reflected in the clear blue water the child saw his own image, and, in the vain endeavour to grasp it, fell into the well.

> 'What is't that fills with wonder
>   The laughing cherub's eyes?
> Why clap his hands with rapture?
>   Why crows he with surprise?
> Within that crystal mirror
>   He views a lovely form—
> Cheeks fair as summer weather—
>   Locks beauteous as the morn.

> 'And wondrous—still more wondrous—
>   While beckoning it to come,
> It with equal love entreats him
>   Into its watery home :—
> Oh, fear! oh, dread!—he clasps it—
>   One cry—and all is o'er;
> The treacherous spring enfolds him—
>   Prince Oswy is no more.'

The anxious princess, his mother, on awaking, traced his footsteps to the spot; and here, in the small mountain pool, with scarcely sufficient water to cover his body, she found her drowned child. The pool is still known as Oswy's Well. His body was in due course borne to the neighbouring churchyard, whither the afflicted mother, killed by grief, was soon afterwards also borne, and laid by his side.

Henceforth the place of their burial was designated—as the place where Oswy-by-his-mother-lay—Osmotherley. The heads of mother and child, carved in stone, are said to be seen still at the east end of the church of the village.

THE GIANT OF SESSAY.

The family who owned Sessay from early times to the days of Henry VII. was that of the Darells. The heirs-male of this family failed in the reign of that king, and the heiress of all the broad lands and manors was a daughter—a strong-minded young woman, named Joan Darell.

About the same time a strange monster began to haunt the woods around the village. He was a huge brute in human form—legs like elephants' legs, arms of a corresponding size, a face most fierce to look upon, with only one eye, placed in the midst of his forehead; a mouth large as a lion's, and garnished with teeth as long as the prongs of a hayfork. His only clothing was a cow's hide fastened across his breast, and with the hair outwards; while over his shoulder he usually carried a stout young tree, torn up by the roots, as a club for offence and defence. Now and then he made the woods ring with demoniacal laughter; now and then with savage, unearthly growls.

Like most giants of olden times, he had a ravenous appetite, and daily he visited the farmers' herds and walked off with a choice heifer or fat ox under his arm, devouring it raw in his forest-cave, which was strewed with bones and horns, etc. If he wanted a change of diet, he paid a visit to the neighbouring miller and left him poorer by a sack of meal, drawn with his long arm through the mill-window. This he took to his cave, and, mixing it in a large trough, with the blood of the animals he had stolen, he ate the porridge thus made with a wonderful relish. But, worst of all, if he wanted a very choice morsel, he would carry off a delicate young maiden from some village home, or a child from the cradle.

This was no pleasant neighbour to have, and the inhabitants, more than once, banded themselves together to destroy him; but all their efforts came to nothing. Either they could not succeed in tracking him to his den, or, if they did, the way in which he showed his enormous teeth, roared out his unearthly growls, or played with the young tree he carried in his hand, had such an effect that his would-be assailants made themselves scarce quicker than they came.

About this time there came a gallant young soldier, who had taken an active part, and done wonderful things, in the wars abroad—Guy, son of Sir John D'Aunay (or Dawney), of Cowick Castle, in South Yorkshire—to pay a visit to Joan Darell, the daughter of his father's old friend at Sessay. He found her occupied in the multifarious business of her large estate and household. One of her difficulties was that of inducing any of her woodmen to go to the woods for the necessary timber for the fuel and repairs. She was trying to persuade one so to do when Dawnay arrived.

'I have heard,' said he, 'of this monster who so terrifies your servants, and devours your tenants' cattle, and even their children. Is it indeed true?'

'Alas!' she replied, 'only too true! But come in and take refreshments.'

Now, young Dawnay had come on an errand at which many young men evince a good deal of nervousness, and beating about the bush. But he went directly to the point, and told the strong-minded spinster, the heiress of all the broad acres of the Darells, that he thought a union of the property of the Darells and Dawnays would serve to build up a great family estate. Would she wed him, and so effect this desirable purpose?

She admired his honesty, and consented on one condition, to prove that he deserved to mate with the last of the Darells.

'Name the condition,' said he. 'I will undertake the task, whatever it may be.'

She replied: 'Slay the monster who is desolating

our fields and spreading such lamentation and woe over the village. Rid us of this brute, and my hand is yours.'

'Willingly will I try,' was the response; 'and if I fall, I shall fall in a good cause.'

'See, there comes the giant!' cried the lady, looking through the window and seeing the monster stalking out of the wood, with his club over his shoulder, towards the mill.

'Truly he is a fearful adversary!' exclaimed the champion, as he joined her at the window and proceeded to buckle on his sword.

On went the giant towards the mill, evidently bent on fetching his usual sack of meal. The miller saw him and trembled, but took no steps to protect his property. The mill was one of those the top of which, with sails, turns on a pivot with the wind. Suddenly, as the giant was drawing the sack out of the window, the wind changed, and swept the sails round to the side on which he was. Round came the arms, or sails, and one of them, catching the monster on the head, sent him stunned on his back to the ground. Young Sir Guy saw his opportunity, ran up, and, before the giant recovered his senses, drove his sword through the brute's one eye into his brain.

There were great rejoicings in all the country round. Next day an immense trench was dug, and the enormous carcase rolled into it and buried, amid shouts of blessing upon the deliverer.

Not many weeks afterwards the bells of Sessay rang merrily at the wedding of Joan Darell and young Sir Guy Dawnay—from whom, I suppose, is descended the respected family of that name, which still, I believe, owns the place.

Now, if this story could be investigated, and traced back step by step to its origin, I have no doubt but that it would be found to be another illustration of the well-known story of 'The Three Crows.'

Either the giant was nothing more than some robber-chief who took up his abode in forest fastnesses and preyed upon the neighbouring inhabitants, or he was some village tyrant who oppressed and annoyed his neighbours, and was got rid of by the Dawnay or some other family of influence; or else—most probable of all, from certain circumstances narrated in the story —he was some unpopular rival for the hand of the heiress of Sessay, and was vanquished, in both love and war, by the more favoured Sir Guy.

I do not suppose the Giant of Sessay was anything worse than one of these; yet popular dislike, and the additions of many repetitions of the story, have made him into the monster I have described.

WADDA OF MULGRAVE, AND BELL, HIS WIFE.

Mulgrave Castle—the seat of the Marquis of Normanby—stands in the parish of Lythe, and three or four miles to the north-west of Whitby. 'At no great distance,' says a writer of the earlier part of the century, 'from the present elegant mansion stand the ruins of an ancient castle, built, according to Camden, 200 years before the Conquest.' Leland thus notices it: 'Mongrave Castle standeth on a craggy hille, and on eche side of it is a hill, far higher than that whereon the castle standeth. The north hille on the top of it hath certain stones, commonely cauli'd Wadde's Grave, whom the people there say to have bene a gigant, and owner of Mongrave.' Wadda, or, as the old writer calls him, Wadde, must have been a marvellous person! A Saxon duke, 'a gigant,' with Bell his 'gigant' wife, the builder of old Mulgrave Castle, Pickering Castle, etc., he is said to have been, and what beyond, who shall say?

One account says that he lived about the end of the eighth, and to the middle of the ninth century, and was one of the conspirators by whom Ethelred, King of Northumberland, was murdered (796 A.D.), and that, to better secure himself against the king's friends, he built, or very much strengthened, the castle at Mulgrave. In building this castle, and that at Pickering, some twenty-two or three miles apart, Wadda and his giantess wife divided the labour—one working at Mulgrave, while the other was busy at Pickering. Unfortunately they had but one hammer for the use of both. This inconvenience, however, was considerably modified by their great physical powers enabling them to perform a feat which must put all modern athletes to the blush. As the hammer was required, at Mulgrave or at Pickering, they threw it backwards and forwards across the country, the only precaution necessary being that the one throwing it should shout to the other to be ready to catch it!

The Roman road, too, which crosses this part of the country, is named Wadde's Causeway, and was formed by them (so says the story) for the convenience of Bell crossing the moor to milk her cow—Wadda doing the paving while his wife brought the stones in her apron.

This occasionally gave way, and the contents falling upon the ground, and Bell disdaining to gather them up again, formed those large heaps of stones yet to be met with among the ling in the neighbourhood. This worthy couple had a son, also called Wadde or Wadda, whose strength was equally as marvellous as that of his parents. One day, when yet little more than an infant, being impatient for his mother's breast, while she was away milking her cow near Swart Hole, he seized an enormous stone, and, in a most unfilial manner, hurled it at her across the valley, and struck her with great violence. She, however, was little hurt, yet so great was the violence with which she was struck that a considerable indentation was made in the stone! This stone remained, so again says the legend, a testimony to the young Wadde's infant prowess, until a few years ago, when it was broken up to mend the highways. One of the rib bones of one of Bell's cows, equal in size to a jawbone of a whale, is said to have been formerly preserved at Mulgrave.

Wadda (and Bell too, it is presumed), being mortal, at length died, and was buried on the hill alluded to by Leland, near his castle of Mulgrave, where two upright stones standing, some years ago, on the spot, twelve feet apart, marked the head and foot of his grave. Whether one or both of them be there now or not the writer knoweth not.

INDEX.

A.

ABBEYS, Legends and Traditions of, 22
Alkelda, St., 19
 churches dedicated to, 10
 martyrdom of, 20
 Well of, 10, 203
Arncliff, Bridge of, 136
Arrows, the Devil's, 115
Athelstane, the King, 80
Augustine, St., mission of, 4

B.

Bargest, etc., Legends of, 126
Baring-Gould, Rev. S., 'Yorkshire Oddities,' 140-142, 150
Barnoldswick Abbey, 59
Battles and Battle-fields, Legends, etc., of, 178
Beamsley, the Three Sisters of, 229
Beggar's Bridge, the, 227
Beverley, St. John of, Legends of, 72
 shrine of, 80
 the Two Sisters of, 76
Blind, eyes given to, 92
 sight given to, 92
Boar, Wild, Legend, 224
Bolling Hall, Legend of, 200
Bolton Priory, Legends, etc., of, 40
Boroughbridge Battle, Legend of, 181
Bosky, or Busky Dyke, Boggard of, 131
Bosky, or Busky Dyke, schoolroom at, 132
Bradford, siege of, 198
 'Pity Poor Bradford,' 198
Bridge, the Broken, at York, 91
Britain, origin of name, 1
Brute the Trojan, 1
Brunnanburg, the Battle of, 83
Buern the Busecarle, 10
Burton, North, Earl Addi's servant of, 79
Burton, South, Puch, the Earl of, 75

C.

Cædmon, the Poet, Legend of, 24
Cashel, the rock of, 119
Churches, sites of, legends of, 119
Claphams, the burial of, 50
Clifford, the Blackfaced, 186
Clifton-cum-Norwood, 18
Coifi, the Druid Arch-priest, 5
Cow, wild, subdued, 109
Crake Castle, Legend of, 8
Crocks of gold, 221
Cromwell, Oliver, and Sir R. Graham 195
Cromwell, Oliver, at Ripley Castle, 196
Cromwell, Oliver, a story of Marston Moor, 197
Cuthbert, St., and Ripon Monastery, 101
Cuthbert, St., fear of, 21

D.

Dacre, Lord, of Gilsland, 188
 daughter of, 225
Danes, the, in Yorkshire, 10
Darrell, family of, 235
Dawnay, family of, 235
Death, presage of, 134
De Espec, Walter, 31
 at Battle of the Standard, 33
Deira, land of, 35
De Lacy, a ballad, 225
De Stuteville, William, 106
Devil's, the, arrows, 115
 Apronful, 124
 Bite, 119
 Bridge, 121
Dibb, or Dibble, the river, 121
Dixon, Dr., 'The Boy of Egremond,' 44
Dixon, Dr., 'The Vision of Seleth,' 61
Dragons, etc., Legends of, 167
Drumming Well, the, of Harpham, 207

Index.

E.
Eboracum, traditions as to origin, 1-3
Ebraucus, 1
Edwin, King of Northumbria, 5
Egremond, the Boy of, 40-44
Ella, King of Bernicia, 10
  death of, 14
Elle-Cross, 17
Ellsworth, 17
Egton, the Beggar's Bridge at, 227
Eskdale, the Hermit of, 27

F.
Filey Brigg, Legend as to Haddocks, 121
Fire, the ordeal of, 93
Fountains, the Abbey of, Legends, etc., of, 29

G.
Giant, the, of Sessay, 235
Giggleswick, the Ebbing and Flowing Well of, 204
Giles, St., Chapel of, 107
Gill Ford, the, 123
Gormire, Legend of, 218
Graham, Sir R., and Cromwell, 195
Grassington, the Bargest near, 129
Gregory and the Youths of Deira, 3
Grimwith Fell, 125

H.
Haddock, the Thumb-mark on, 121
Handale, the Serpent of, 168
Harpham, the Wells at, 207
Hart-leap Well, the, 209
Haverah Park—
  a Lame Legend, 223
  a Wild Boar Legend, 224
  De Lacy and Lord Dacre's daughter, 225
Heathen Temple at Godmundham, 6
Hedley, the monks of, 105
Helen, St., Well of, 203, 206
Hermit, the, of Eskdale, 27
Hermit, St. Robert the, 104
Hilda, St., Worms of, 23
  Obeisance of Birds to, 24
Horse, the White, of the Strid, 229
Hylda, St., the Hermitage of, 105
Hylda, the Nun of Nun-Appleton, 66

I.
Ilkley, Cow and Calf Rocks near, 125
Iseur, 3, 116
Ivo, the Jew, 109

J.
John, St., of Beverley, miracles of, 72
  Well of, 207
Jordan, the, of England, 7

K.
Kaer-Ebrauc, 1
Kirkham Priory, Legends, etc., of, 31
Kirkham, Prior of, the horse of, 36
Kirkstall Abbey, Legends, etc., of, 59
  'The Vision of Seleth,' 61
Knaresbrough, St. Robert of, Legends of, 104

L.
Lady, Our, Wells of, 205
Lady Well at Thirsk, 206
Lakes, etc., Legends, etc., of, 202
Lame Legend, a, 223
Lancaster, Thomas, Earl of, 181, 182
Leake Church, site of, 120
Lister, Captain, and the gravedigger, 198
Littondale, the Wise Woman of, 134
Loaning, Chop Head, poem of, 183
Loschy Wood, the Dragon of, 170
Lovers' Bridge, the, 227
Lucas, Mr. Joseph, F.G.S., 129

M.
Margaret, St., Well of, 203
'Mary, the Maid of the Inn,' 62
Marston Moor Fight, Traditions, etc., of, 194
Marston Moor Fight, Oliver Cromwell and Sir R. Graham, 195
Marston Moor Fight, Oliver Cromwell at Ripley, 196
Marston Moor Fight, another story of, 197
Mauleverers, the burials of, 50
Meaux or Melsa Abbey, Legend of, 37
Meaux or Melsa Abbey, Chronicle of, 39
Miscellaneous Legends, etc., 219
Monmouth, Geoffrey of, 1
Mother Shipton, Legends, etc., of, 151
  Death of, 156
  Apocryphal Sayings of, 164
  Prophecies of, 156
Mulgrave, Wadda, the giant of, 239
Mungo, St., Well of, 203
Myton, Battle of, 178

N.
Nortons, the fate of, 46
Northallerton, an army stopped near, 21
Northumbria, the conversion of, 5
Nun-Appleton, Hylda, the nun of, 66
Nunnington Church, 171
Nursa Knot, rocks, 124

O.
Ord, J. W., ballad by, 234
Osbert, King of Northumbria, 11

Osmotherley, Legend of, 233
Osnaburg, mountain, 234
Otterington, North, site of church, 120
Ould, E. A., poem by, 144

P.

Palmer, the Grey, Legend of, 66
Paulinus, St., in Northumbria, 4
Phillips, Mrs. S. K., poems by, 183, 216
Pockstones, rocks, 125

Q.

Quintin, St., family of, and the Drumming Well, 208

R.

Ragnar Lodbrog, Legend of, 8
Rievaulx Abbey, Legends, etc., of, 31
Ripley Castle and Oliver Cromwell, 196
Ripon, Monastery of, and St. Cuthbert, 101
Rising in the North, the, 46
Robert, St., of Knaresborough, Legends of, 104
Robert, St., of Knaresborough, chapel of, 107
Robert, St., of Knaresborough, cave of, 109
Robert, St., of Knaresborough, death of, 113
Roche Abbey, Legend of, 70
Rogers, poem by, 41
Roseberry Topping, mountain, 234
Roulstone Scar, 116
Rutland, Edmund, Earl of, 184
Rylstone, White Doe of, 45

S.

Satanic Agency, Legends of, 115
Saxton Church, 188
Selby Abbey, Legend of, 65
Seleth the Hermit, the Vision of, 61
Semerwater, Legends of, 214
Sessay, the Giant of, 62
Sexhow, the Worm of, 169
Shipton, Mother, Legends, etc., of, 151
Shipton, Mother, Apocryphal Sayings of, 164
Shipton, Mother, death of, 156
Prophecies of, 156
Slingsby, the Serpent of, 172
Sockburn, the tenure of the Manor of, 166
Southey's 'Mary, the Maid of the Inn,' 62
Stags, tamed, 110
Standard, the Battle of, 33

Strid, the Boy of Egremond at the, 41
the White Horse of the, 229
Student, the young, 95
Swale, the river, 7
Swine Harrie, the, 219
Sword, the pledged, 80

T.

Tadcaster, the Battle of, 198
Thirsk, the Lady Well at, 206
Thorpe-sub-Montem, hamlet of, 122
Towton, Battle of, 187
Red and White Roses, Legend of, 189
Towton, Red and White Roses, ballads of, 190, 191
Traumar Reid, Legends of York by, 97
Troller's Gill, the Bargest of, 126

U.

Ulphus, the Horn of, 96
Upsall, Castle of, 181-183
the Crocks of Gold of, 221

W.

Wadda, the Giant of Mulgrave, 239
Wakefield, the Battle of, 184
Wantley, the Dragon of, 173
ballad of, 174
Watton Nunnery, Legend of, 73
Wells, Legends, etc., of, 200
dedicated to Saints, 203
Lady, 205
Well, the Ebbing and Flowing, 204
St. Helen's, 206
the Hart-leap, 209
the Drumming, 207
St. John's, 207
Worship, 203
Whitby Abbey, Legends, etc., of, 22
the bells of, 29
Wigstones, rocks, 124
William, St., of York, Legends, etc., of, 86
William, St., of York, window of, 89
Winwaedfield, fight of, 23
Wordsworth's 'Force of Prayer,' 42
'White Doe of Rylstone,' 45
'Hart-leap Well,' 209

Y.

York, the Broken Bridge at, 91
Minster, foundation of, 7
Origin of the name, 1
Ghost at Trinity Church, 140
Richard, Duke of, 184
St. William of, 86
Yorkshire, Early History of, 1

Elliot Stock, Paternoster Row, London.

INTERNATIONAL FOLKLORE
An Arno Press Collection

Allies, Jabez. **On The Ancient British, Roman, and Saxon Antiquities and Folk-Lore of Worcestershire.** 1852

Blair, Walter and Franklin J. Meine, editors. **Half Horse Half Alligator.** 1956

Bompas, Cecil Henry, translator. **Folklore of the Santal Parganas.** 1909

Bourne, Henry. **Antiquitates Vulgares; Or, The Antiquities of the Common People.** 1725

Briggs, Katharine Mary. **The Anatomy of Puck.** 1959

Briggs, Katharine Mary. **Pale Hecate's Team.** 1962

Brown, Robert. **Semitic Influence in Hellenic Mythology.** 1898

Busk, Rachel Harriette. **The Folk-Songs of Italy.** 1887

Carey, George. **A Faraway Time and Place.** 1971

Christiansen, Reidar Th. **The Migratory Legends.** 1958

Clouston, William Alexander. **Flowers From a Persian Garden, and Other Papers.** 1890

Colcord, Joanna Carver. **Sea Language Comes Ashore.** 1945

Dorson, Richard Mercer, editor. **Davy Crockett.** 1939

Douglas, George Brisbane, editor. **Scottish Fairy and Folk Tales.** 1901

Gaidoz, Henri and Paul Sébillot. **Blason Populaire De La France.** 1884

Gardner, Emelyn Elizabeth. **Folklore From the Schoharie Hills, New York.** 1937

Gill, William Wyatt. **Myths and Songs From The South Pacific.** 1876

Gomme, George Laurence. **Folk-Lore Relics of Early Village Life.** 1883

Grimm, Jacob and Wilhelm. **Deutsche Sagen.** 1891

Gromme, Francis Hindes. **Gypsy Folk-Tales.** 1899

Hambruch, Paul. **Faraulip.** 1924

Ives, Edward Dawson. **Larry Gorman.** 1964

Jansen, William Hugh. **Abraham "Oregon" Smith.** 1977

Jenkins, John Geraint. **Studies in Folk Life.** 1969

Kingscote, Georgiana and Pandit Natêsâ Sástrî, compilers. **Tales of the Sun.** 1890

Knowles, James Hinton. **Folk-Tales of Kashmir.** 1893

Lee, Hector Haight. **The Three Nephites.** 1949

MacDougall, James, compiler. **Folk Tales and Fairy Lore in Gaelic and English.** 1910

Mather, Increase. **Remarkable Providences Illustrative of the Earlier Days of American Colonisation.** 1856

McNair, John F.A. and Thomas Lambert Barlow. **Oral Tradition From the Indus.** 1908

McPherson, Joseph McKenzie. **Primitive Beliefs in the North-East of Scotland.** 1929

Miller, Hugh. **Scenes and Legends of the North of Scotland.** 1869

Müller, Friedrich Max. **Comparative Mythology.** 1909

Palmer, Abram Smythe. **The Samson-Saga and Its Place in Comparative Religion.** 1913

Parker, Henry. **Village Folk-Tales of Ceylon.** Three volumes. 1910-1914

Parkinson, Thomas. **Yorkshire Legends and Traditions.** 1888

Perrault, Charles. **Popular Tales.** 1888

Rael, Juan B. **Cuentos Españoles de Colorado y Nuevo Méjico.** Two volumes. 1957

Ralston, William Ralston Shedden. **Russian Folk-Tales.** 1873

Rhys Davids, Thomas William, translator. **Buddhist Birth Stories; Or, Jātaka Tales.** 1880

Ricks, George Robinson. **Some Aspects of the Religious Music of the United States Negro.** 1977

Swynnerton, Charles. **Indian Nights' Entertainment, Or Folk-Tales From the Upper Indus.** 1892

Sydow, Carl Wilhelm von. **Selected Papers on Folklore.** 1948

Taliaferro, Harden E. **Fisher's River (North Carolina) Scenes and Characters.** 1859

Temple, Richard Carnac. **The Legends of the Panjâb.** Three volumes. 1884-1903

Tully, Marjorie F. and Juan B. Rael. **An Annotated Bibliography of Spanish Folklore in New Mexico and Southern Colorado.** 1950

Wratislaw, Albert Henry, translator. **Sixty Folk-Tales From Exclusively Slavonic Sources.** 1889

Yates, Norris W. **William T. Porter and the Spirit of the Times.** 1957